Dwayne's Guitar Lessons Presents:

Learn to Play the Pentatonic Scales

A Guide to Lead Guitar Mastery

By
Guitar Teacher
Dwayne Jenkins

Introduction

Welcome to Learn to Play the Pentatonic Scales. An immersive exploration into the world of lead guitar playing. This guide is designed for those who are eager to enhance their skills and expand their musical vocabulary.

The pentatonic scale is a cornerstone of modern music, renowned for its simplicity and versatility. With only five notes, this scale lays the foundation for countless memorable riffs, solos, and melodies across a wide range of genres.

Learn to Play the Pentatonic Scales is structured to provide a comprehensive learning experience, combining theoretical knowledge with practical exercises. Each chapter builds on the previous one.

You'll explore a variety of techniques, from essential scales and fingerings to advanced improvisation and performance preparation. Along the way, quizzes and summaries reinforce key concepts, ensuring a solid grasp of the material.

As you advance your skills and delve deeper into the world of lead guitar, remember that the journey itself is as rewarding as the destination. Each new technique you master and every challenge you overcome, adds to your unique musical identity.

Embrace the incremental progress and celebrate your achievements, no matter how small they may seem. This mindset will not only keep you motivated but also make the learning process more satisfying and enjoyable.

Your passion for music is your greatest asset. It fuels your creativity, drives your practice, and connects you with others who share your love for the guitar. Keep this passion alive by constantly seeking inspiration from diverse sources.

Dive into this guide with an open mind and a willingness to practice daily. As you embark on this musical journey, you'll discover new dimensions of your guitar playing, unlocking the full potential of the pentatonic scale and beyond. Good luck, and don't forget to have fun.

Sincerely, Dwayne Jenkins

Table of Contents

Chapter I: Understanding the Basics

Lesson 1: What is the Pentatonic Scale?

The pentatonic scale is a five-note scale that forms the foundation of many musical genres, including rock, blues, and pop. Its simplicity and versatility make it an essential tool for lead guitarists.

Unlike the more complex seven-note scales, the pentatonic scale omits the fourth and seventh degrees of the major, creating a sound that is both familiar and distinctly melodic.

Major vs. Minor Pentatonic

The minor pentatonic scale flattens the third and seventh notes of the major scale, omitting the second and sixth degrees. Understanding the difference between the major and minor pentatonic scales is crucial for effective guitar playing.

The major pentatonic scale has a bright, uplifting sound, whereas the minor pentatonic scale has a darker, more soulful tone. Both can be found in blues, jazz, and rock music.

2

Dy mastering both the major and minor pentatonic scales, you can confidently navigate various musical styles and create compelling solos while adding to your scale vocabulary.

The Major Scale: 1 2 3 4 5 6 7 = seven notes

The Major Pentatonic Scale: 1 2 3 5 6 = five notes

The Minor Pentatonic Scale: 1 b3 4 5 b7 = five notes

Can you see how the two pentatonic scales take out the two notes previously mentioned to create two new scales?

The Major Scale: 1 2 3 4 5 6 7

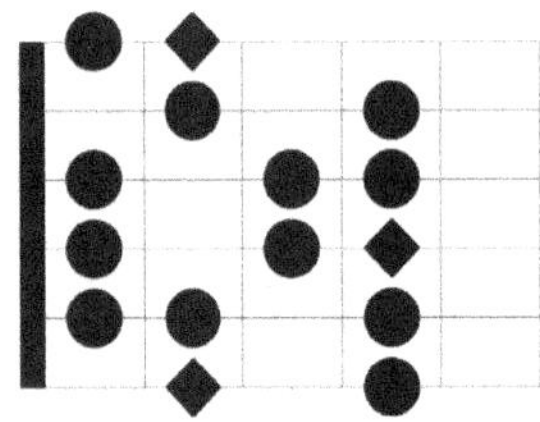

The Major Pentatonic Scale: 1 2 3 5 6

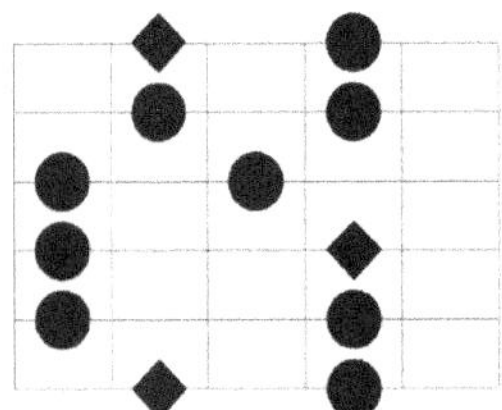

The Minor Pentatonic Scale: 1 b3 4 5 b7

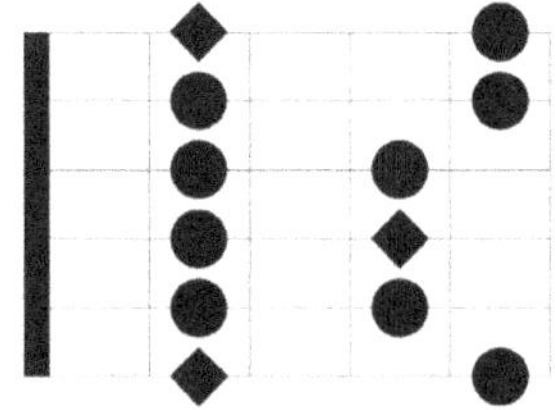

By studying these diagrams, you'll be able to see how the elimination of two notes to make up these two additional scales alters their note pattern. As well as making them easier to play. Notice the difference between the major pentatonic scale and the regular major scale.

You can also see that out of the three scale patterns, the minor pentatonic is the easiest to play by the way the notes line up across the fretboard. That is why this one is the most popular.

You start with the major, which is the foundation for all chords and scales, then move to the minor pentatonic because of its ease of playability.

This makes them work over many chords and progressions in both major and minor keys, allowing for ease of improvisation, and all the rock guitar masters use them—Jimi Hendrix, Jimmy Page, SRV, Slash, Van Halen, etc., etc., etc.

4

Lesson 2: Fingering and Technique

Mastering finger placement is vital for smooth and efficient guitar playing. This not only enhances your ability to play clean notes but also minimizes tension and prevents strain.

Tips For Proper Finger Placement

1. **Curve Your Fingers:** Ensure that your fingers are curved with the tips pressing down on the strings. This helps produce clear tones and allows more control over the strings.

2. **Use Your Fingertips:** Press down on the strings with the very tips of your fingers to avoid muting adjacent strings. This technique will help you transition between notes more smoothly.

3. **Stay Close to the Frets**: Position your fingers close to the fret without touching it. This reduces the effort required to press the string down and prevents buzzing.

Use these three tips to set up a solid foundation for finger placement. This will make a huge difference later down the line when you start learning soloing techniques.

Smooth Transitions Between Notes

To play fluid solos and maintain the flow of your music, it's essential to practice seamless transitions between notes. Here are some techniques to help you achieve smooth transitions:

1. **Economy of Motion:** Minimize the movement of your fingers by keeping them close to the strings. This will help you move quickly and effortlessly from one note to another.
2. **Practice Slowly:** Begin by practicing scales and patterns at a slow tempo, focusing on accuracy and precision. Gradually increase the speed as you become more comfortable.
3. **Use a Metronome:** A metronome can help you maintain consistent timing and gradually increase your speed while keeping transitions smooth.

By focusing on these concepts, you'll build a solid foundation for more advanced soloing techniques.

Lesson 3: Rhythm and Timing

Understanding rhythm and timing is fundamental to becoming a proficient lead guitarist. These elements are essential for building a steady foundation and ensuring that your solos and riffs fit seamlessly into the broader musical context.

Keeping Time

Maintaining a consistent rhythm is crucial for any guitarist. Here are some strategies to help you keep time effectively:

1. **Use a Metronome:** Practice with a metronome to develop a strong sense of timing. Start at a slower tempo and gradually increase it as you become more comfortable.
2. **Count Out Loud:** While playing, count the beats out loud to internalize the rhythm. This practice can help you stay on track, especially when playing complex rhythms.
3. **Subdivision Practice:** Break down beats into more minor subdivisions (e.g., eighth notes or sixteenth notes) to improve your precision and timing.

Working With a Metronome

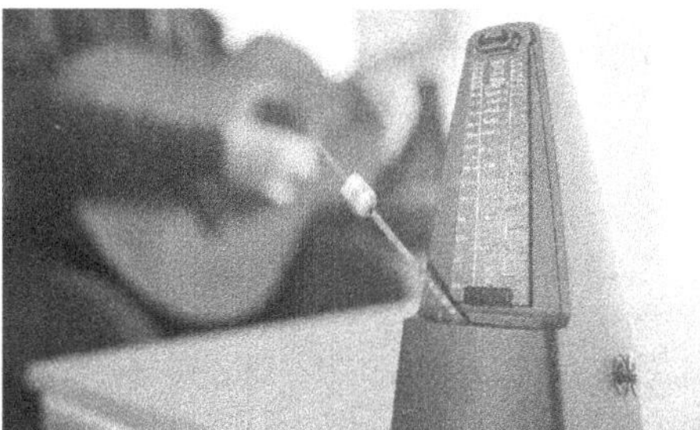

There is no better way to develop timing and rhythm than by working with a metronome. This type of activity builds the internal clock that every musician needs. So, don't overlook this fundamental concept.

Counting out loud and subdivision practices are an excellent way to build a solid foundation for developing rhythm and timing. Now, if you're not too keen on counting out loud, perfectly understandable, just do it internally.

Syncopation Techniques

Syncopation involves placing emphasis on beats or parts of beats that are typically unaccented, creating rhythmic interest and variety. Here are a few techniques to incorporate syncopation into your playing:

1. **Offbeat Accents:** Practice accentuating notes that fall on the offbeat. This technique can add an unexpected twist to your rhythms.
2. **Rhythmic Displacement:** Shift your phrases by starting them on different beats, which can create tension and release within your music.
3. **Dynamic Variation:** Use changes in volume to highlight syncopated notes, making them stand out more prominently in your playing.

By mastering rhythm and timing, you'll be able to play with greater confidence and creativity, ensuring that your solos are both technically sound and musically expressive. These skills are invaluable for any guitarist looking to enhance their lead playing abilities.

Chapter I Quiz

In Chapter 1, we covered the basics. These are what will develop your foundation. Get this right, and all else will fall into place.

Q: Why is the pentatonic scale different from the major scale?
A: ____

Q: What makes the minor scale different from the major?
A: ____

Q: Why is proper finger placement important for playing guitar?
A: ____

Q: What helps achieve smooth transitions between notes?
A: ____

Q: What tool can help you develop proper timing in rhythm?
A: ____

Q: What is the benefit of playing syncopated rhythms?
A: ____

Chapter I Summary

First, you have the pentatonic scale. A five-note scale that forms the foundation of many musical styles. Including rock, blues, jazz, and pop. Making it an essential tool for lead guitarists to create riffs, solos, and melody lines.

Second, you have both major and minor pentatonic scales. The major scale eliminates the fourth and seventh, and the minor scale eliminates the second and sixth. Creating a simpler, easier scale pattern to navigate.

Third, mastering finger placement is vital to smooth, efficient guitar playing. Enhancing your ability to play clean notes while minimizing tension and preventing strain.

Fourth, understanding rhythm and timing. These elements are essential for becoming a proficient lead guitarist, building a solid foundation, and ensuring that your solos fit seamlessly within the musical context.

Lastly, practice with a metronome to develop a strong sense of timing and rhythm. Maintaining a sense of rhythm is crucial for any guitar player and must be accomplished.

Chapter II: Scale Mastery

Lesson 4: The Major Pentatonic Scale

To fully harness the power of the major pentatonic scale, it's essential to learn its five positions across the guitar neck. Each position offers unique tonal possibilities and enables fluid movement between different areas of the fretboard.

The reason there are five patterns is that each one is based on a tone degree.

Ex: C Major Pentatonic = C D E G A

Pattern 1 will start on the C note, pattern 2 will start on the D note, pattern 3 will start on the E note, pattern 4 will start on the G note, and pattern 5 will start on the A note.

These are all made up of the same five notes, but because they all start on different tone degrees, they each have a slightly different character.

Let's take a look at the five major entatonic scales. Remember, these will be the same in any key you play them in.

The Five Major Pentatonic Scales

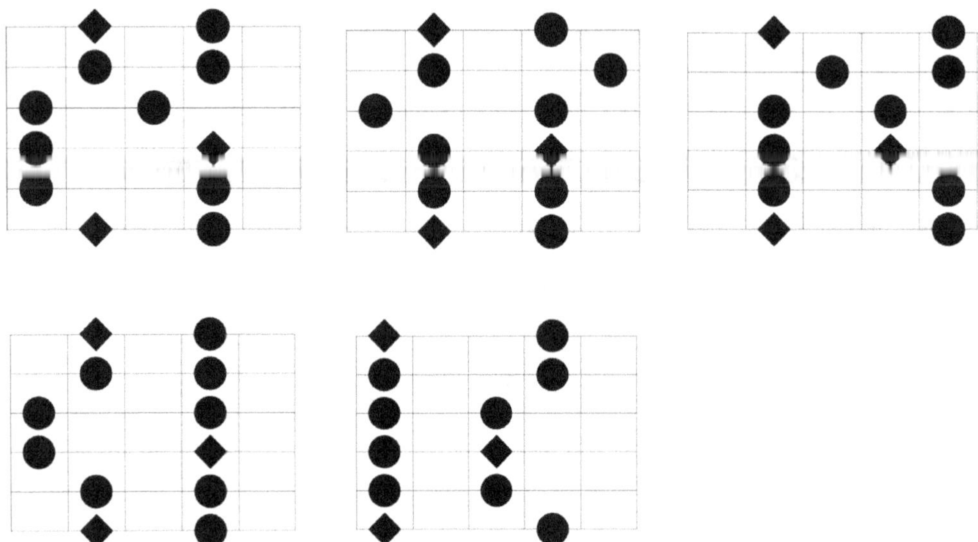

All of these start on a scale tone degree of the key they come out of. The diamond shape indicates the root note. If these were played in the key of C major as mentioned before, each of these scale patterns would start on one of those notes.

Pattern 1 would be at the 8th fret (C note) on the 6th string.

Pattern 2 would be at the 10th fret (D note) on the 6th string.

Pattern 3 would be at the 12th fret (E note) on the 6th string.

Pattern 4 would be at the 15th fret (G note) on the 6th string.

Pattern 5 would be at the 17th fret (A note) on the 6th string.

*Patterns 4 and 5 could also be played at the 3rd and 5th frets.

Once you have mastered each position individually, the next step is to connect them fluidly across the neck. This ability will enhance your improvisational skills and enable you to create longer, more expressive solos.

- **Practice Transitions:** Move smoothly between positions by practicing note and phrase connections.
- **Use Slides and Bends:** Incorporate techniques to transition between positions naturally, adding emotion and style to your playing.
- **Explore Different Keys:** Apply these positions in various keys to become versatile and adaptable in any musical situation.

By mastering the major pentatonic scale's five positions and learning to connect them, you'll gain the ability to navigate the fretboard with confidence and creativity, allowing for dynamic and engaging guitar solos.

Remember, these are always in the same order, no matter what key you play them in. You can play them on any fret and any string, but I recommend starting on the 6th string first to get familiar with them.

14

Lesson 5: The Minor Pentatonic Scale

The minor pentatonic also has five scale patterns that span the guitar neck, just like the major. With each offering a unique tonal quality.

The 5 Minor Pentatonic Scale Patterns

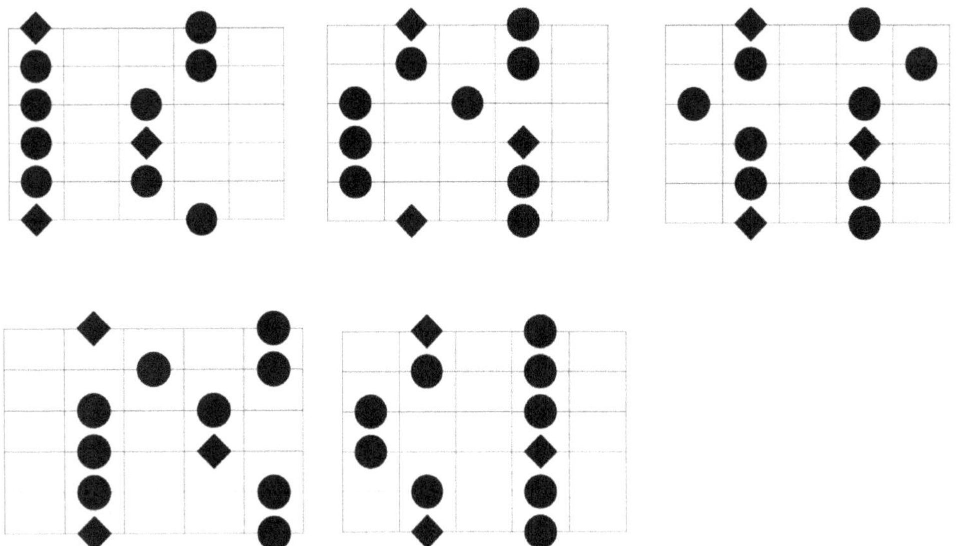

If you were in the key of A minor, A, C, D, E, and G, each pattern would start on one of these notes. The A at the 5th fret, 6th string, the C at the 8th, the D at the 10th, the E at the 12th, and the G at the 15th or 3rd fret.

If you are in the Key of G minor, the patterns would start on the notes in that key. The same thing goes for E minor, B minor, and every other minor.

Here are a few examples:

G Minor Pentatonic = G A# C D F

G = Pattern1, A# = Pattern 2, C = Pattern 3, D = Pattern 4, F = Pattern 5.

E Minor Pentatonic = E G A B D

E = Pattern 1, G = Pattern 2, A = Pattern 3, B = Pattern 4, D = Pattern 5.

B Minor Pentatonic = B D E F# A

B = Pattern 1, D = Pattern 2, E = Pattern 3, F# = Pattern 4, A = Pattern 5.

Remember, the notes within the scale tell you where each of the five patterns will be located. Once you know the notes, the patterns will be easy to find.

Also, the patterns always follow the same order. Making them a lot easier to learn and master.

Once you master each pattern individually, it's crucial to connect them like you did the majors. This capability will enhance your improvisational skills and your fretboard knowledge.

- **Practice Seamless Transitions:** Work on moving between patterns fluently by practicing connecting notes and phrases across the fretboard.
- **Incorporate solo techniques:** Use them to transition between patterns, adding emotional depth and fluidity to your playing.
- **Experiment with Different Keys:** Apply these patterns in various keys to become a versatile player, capable of adapting to any musical context.

By mastering the minor pentatonic scale's five patterns and learning to shift between them, you'll gain the ability to traverse the fretboard with ease and creativity, crafting compelling and dynamic guitar solos.

By mastering the major and minor pentatonic scale patterns, you set yourself up to be able to play within any major or minor key, or solo over any major or minor chord progression.

Lesson 6: Common Pentatonic Runs

The pentatonic scale is not only foundational but also provides endless possibilities for creating fast, exciting, and melodically engaging runs. Mastering these runs can significantly enhance your lead guitar playing, allowing you to impress with speed and creativity.

Building Speed

Developing speed in your playing requires focused practice and the proper techniques. Here are some strategies to help you build speed while maintaining accuracy:

- **Alternate Picking:** Use alternate picking (down-and-up strokes) to ensure a consistent, efficient motion. This technique is crucial for achieving speed without sacrificing precision.

A technique that will be developed in the upcoming lessons. This is how you will build speed and articulation.

- **Finger Independence:** Practice exercises that promote finger independence, enabling each finger to move quickly and accurately. This can be achieved through finger drills and repetitive scale patterns.
- **Gradual Tempo Increase:** Start practicing your runs at a comfortable, slow tempo. Gradually increase the speed as you become more relaxed, ensuring that you maintain clarity at every tempo.

Finger independence and controlling tempo will be the foundation of your lead guitar playing.

Creating Melodic Lines

While speed can be impressive, integrating melodic elements into your runs makes them musically engaging. Here are some tips for crafting melodic pentatonic runs:

- **Use Phrasing:** Break your runs into smaller phrases rather than playing continuous notes. This approach adds structure and musicality to your runs.

Phrasing is essential to lead guitar playing, so make sure you master this concept.

- **Incorporate Dynamics:** Vary the volume and intensity of your playing to add emotion and interest. Dynamics can help emphasize specific notes and create a more captivating performance.
- **Blend Techniques:** Combine different techniques such as slides, bends, and hammer-ons within your runs. This variety keeps your lines fresh and exciting.

Dynamics and techniques such as string bending will be how you add emotion to the notes of the scales. It's not enough to just know the notes or where to play them; you want to be able to use them to paint beautiful musical landscapes.

Exploring Pentatonic Variations

To add even more depth and variety to your pentatonic runs, consider exploring variations of the scale:

- **Extended Pentatonic Scale:** Expand beyond the standard five-note scale by including additional passing tones. This creates a more complex and nuanced sound, opening up new melodic possibilities.

This will give you more options to expand your ideas.

- **Pentatonic Octaves:** Experiment with the octaves of the pentatonic scale by starting your runs on one octave and juming ot the next. This approach can alter the mood and feel of your runs, providing fresh, creative avenues.
- **Hybrid Scales.** Integrate elements from other scales, such as the blues scale or major scale, with your pentatonic runs. This blending can create unique and unexpected musical textures.

Utilizing octave jumps and elements from other scales are both common in the lead guitar landscape and should be mastered for effective melodic playing.

By mastering common pentatonic runs, you'll be prepared to incorporate speed and melody into your solos, enhancing your overall guitar playing and musical expression.

These skills will enable you to captivate audiences with both technical prowess and artistic flair, as well as improve your mastery of the fretboard.

Chapter II Quiz

In Chapter 2, you have learned about scale mastery. Both major and minor pentatonic scales. The five patterns of each and the standard scale run.

Q: What is the tonal quality of the major pentatonic scale?
A: ____

Q: What is the benefit of learning all five scale patterns?
A: ____

Q: What genre commonly uses the minor pentatonic scale?
A: ____

Q: What's an essential step in mastering the minor pentatonic?
A: ____

Q: How do pentatonic runs help you to build speed?
A: ____

Q: How can you add melodic interest to your pentatonic runs?
A: ____

Chapter II Summary

First, to fully harness the power of the major pentatonic scale, you need to learn its five scale patterns across the fretboard. With each offering a unique tonal possibility.

Second, these all start on a tone degree of the scale they come out of. The five notes to the pentatonic scale (major and minor) will each have their own specific pattern.

Third, the minor pentatonic scale, just like the major, also has five patterns that span the fretboard. These will also start on each tone degree just like the majors do. Each offering a unique tonal quality.

Fourth, the pentatonic scale not only provides a solid foundation but also offers a simple framework for melodic, engaging runs. Mastering these can help you build speed and develop accuracy.

Lastly, add soloing techniques such as slides, bends, alternate picking, and dynamics. Allowing your pentatonic scales and runs to capture your audience with technical prowess and artistic flair.

Chapter III: Soloing Techniques

Lesson 7: Hammer-ons and Pull-offs

Hammer-ons and pull-offs are fundamental techniques in lead guitar playing, enabling fluid, connected notes with minimal picking. These techniques will allow you to execute rapid sequences and embellishments.

Mastering Hammer-Ons

A hammer-on involves striking a note on the fretboard without picking it. This technique creates a smooth transition between notes and is essential for building speed and fluidity.

- **Basic Technique:** Start by picking a note, then quickly "hammer" onto a higher note on the exact string using another finger. Make sure that the hammered note rings clearly and is as loud as the initially picked note.

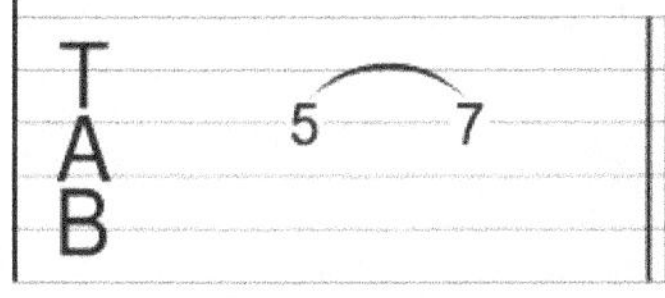

Example of a hammer-on technique.

- **Strength and Accuracy:** Practice hammer-ons with different fingers to build strength and dexterity. Please focus on accuracy to make sure the hammered note is clean and distinct.
- **Exercise:** Play a series of hammer-ons across the fretboard, starting slowly and gradually increasing speed. Use a metronome to maintain consistent timing.

Perfecting Pull-Offs

The pull-off technique complements hammer-ons by allowing a note to sound as you remove a finger from the fretboard. This technique creates a seamless transition to a lower note.

- **Basic Technique:** Begin with a fretted note, then "pull off" to a lower note by slightly pulling the string with your fretting finger. This should produce a clear sound without additional picking.

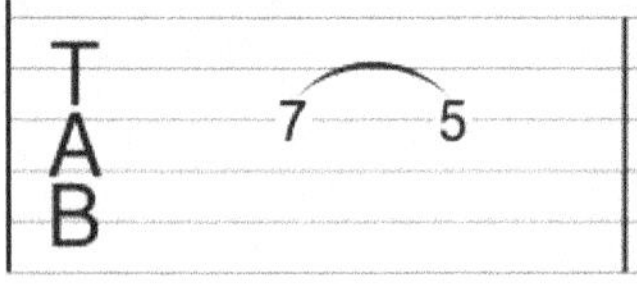

Example of a pull-off.

- **Volume Consistency:** Ensure the pulled-off note maintains volume comparable to the initial note, creating a smooth, even transition.
- **Exercise:** Practice pull-offs across various strings and positions, focusing on preserving volume and clarity. Gradually incorporate pull-offs into scale runs and melodic lines.

Combining Hammer-Ons and Pull-Offs

Once comfortable with each technique individually, combine hammer-ons and pull-offs to create fast, fluid musical phrases.

- **Legato Runs:** Practice combining hammer-ons and pull-offs in legato runs, where notes are played smoothly without re-picking. This technique is ideal for creating seamless, flowing lines.
- **Building Speed:** Use these techniques to increase speed in your solos. Practice slowly at first, focusing on accuracy, then gradually increase tempo.

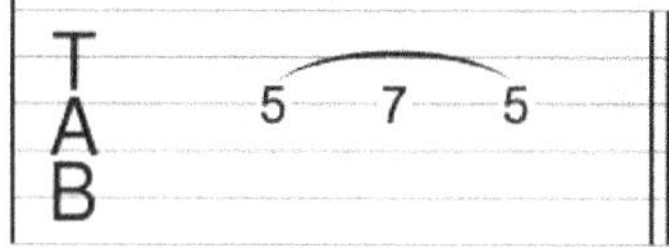

Example of a hammer-on, pull-off.

- **Incorporating Into Solos:** Integrate hammer-ons and pull-offs into your solos to add expressiveness and complexity. These techniques allow for rapid sequences and embellishments that captivate listeners.

Hammer-ons

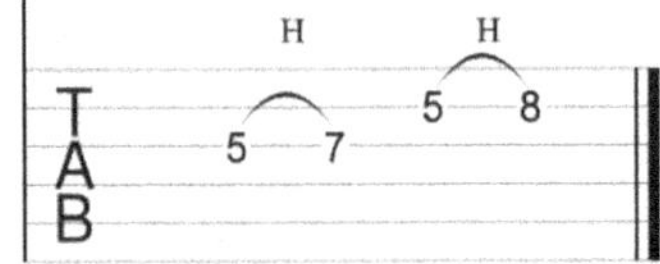

Pull-offs

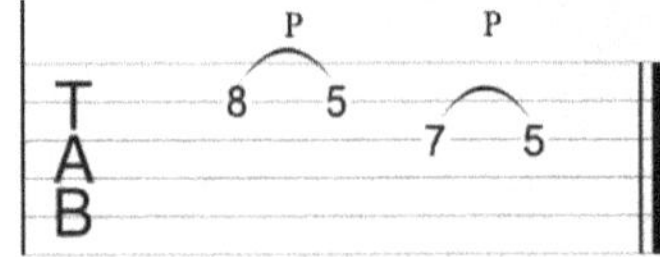

Hammer-on, pull-off sequence

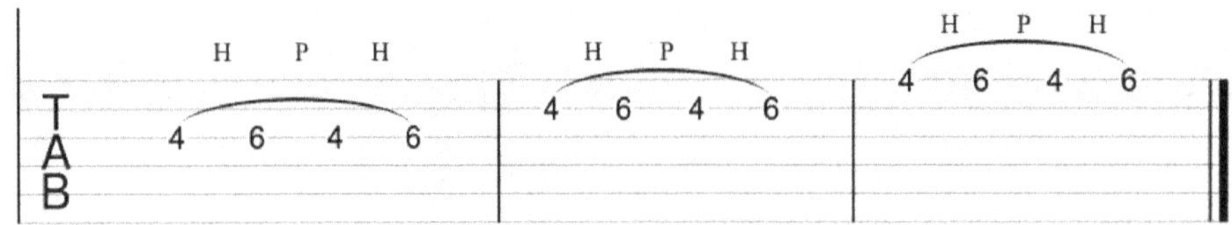

By mastering hammer-ons and pull-offs, you'll enhance your ability to play fluid, connected notes and add dynamic expression to your lead guitar playing.

Lesson 8: Slides, Bends, and Vibrato

Slides, bends, and vibrato are essential techniques that add expressiveness and personality to your guitar playing. Mastering these techniques will allow you to create solos that are not only technically impressive but also emotionally compelling.

Mastering Slides

Slides involve moving a finger along the string to transition smoothly between notes. This technique can add fluidity and a vocal-like quality to your playing.

- **Basic Technique:** Start by fretting a note, then maintain pressure as you slide your finger up or down the neck to another fret. Make sure the transition is smooth and the second note rings clearly.

Here are examples of guitar slides. A great way to express notes within the scales.

- **Dircotional Slides:** Practice slides both ascending and descending to create different emotional effects. Ascending slides can build tension, while descending slides often resolve phrases.

- **Slide Combinations:** Combine slides with other techniques, such as hammer-ons or pull-offs, to create intricate, expressive lines. This combination can add complexity and flair to your playing.

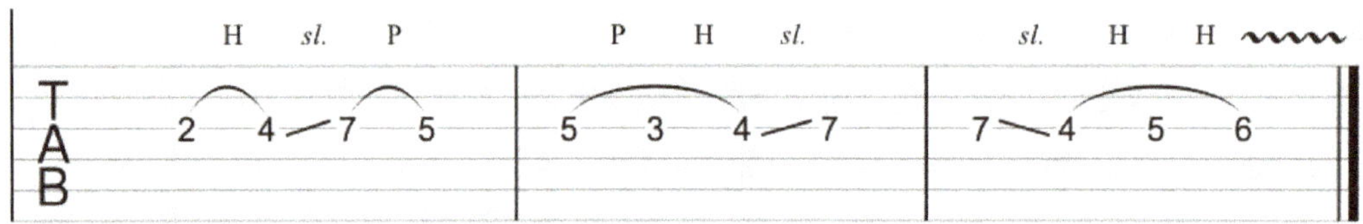

Here is an example of all three techniques together. Slides, Hammer-ons, and pull-offs. This is how guitar licks are created.

Perfecting Bends

Bends are a powerful tool for adding emotion and intensity to your solos. They mimic the human voice's ability to express longing, joy, or sorrow.

- **Basic Technique:** Start by playing a note, then push or pull the string across the fretboard to raise the pitch. Use your wrist and arm for support and control to ensure the bend reaches the intended pitch.

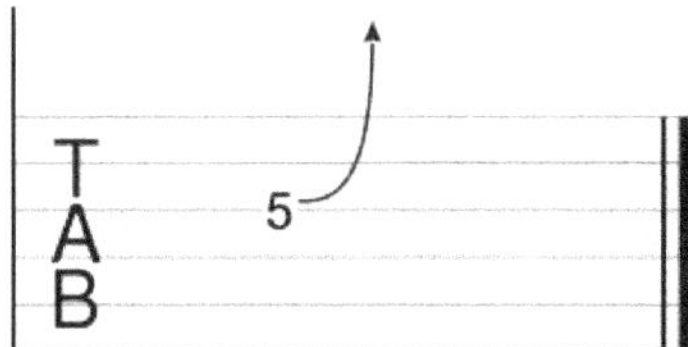 Example of a string bend.

- **Half- and Whole-Step Bends:** Practice bending notes by both half- and whole-step intervals. Each type of bend creates a different sound and emotional effect, expanding your expressive palette.
- **Bend Releases:** Learn to bend a note, then release the bend smoothly. This technique can add a dramatic touch to your playing and surprise your audience.

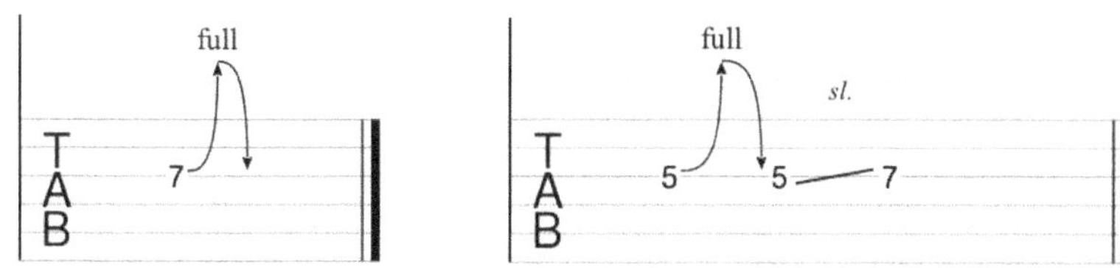

Here is a bend release, and a bend release with a slide up.

Exploring Vibrato

Vibrato is a subtle yet impactful technique that adds richness and sustain to notes. It involves oscillating the pitch of a note slightly to create a warm, singing tone.

- **Basic Technique:** Start by playing a note, then use your wrist to rock your finger back and forth, creating a slight variation in pitch. Keep the movement controlled to ensure the vibrato is smooth and even.

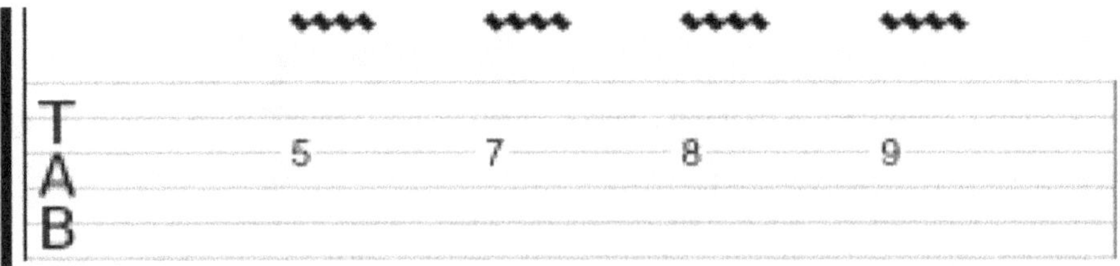

Here is an example of vibrato on four different notes on the 3rd string. Play the note and slightly vibrate it up and down.

This is a very personal technique and takes a bit of practice. So work this into your daily routine to master it. It is a great way to express a note.

- **Wide vs. Narrow Vibrato:** Experiment with the width of your vibrato. A wide vibrato involves larger pitch variations, adding drama and intensity, while a narrow vibrato is more subtle and gentle.
- **Speed Variation:** Vary the speed of your vibrato to match the mood of the music. Faster vibrato adds urgency, while slower vibrato can convey calmness or introspection.

Integrating Slides, Bends, and Vibrato

By integrating slides, bends, and vibrato into your playing, you can create solos that resonate with listeners and convey deep emotion.

- **Expressive Phrasing:** Use these techniques to enhance the emotional impact of your phrases. Consider the story you want to tell with your music and choose the technique that best conveys that narrative.
- **Combine Techniques:** Blend slides, bends, and vibrato within a single phrase or note to add layers of expression and complexity to your playing.

Use concepts like these to get the most out of using vibrato.

Dend with vibrato

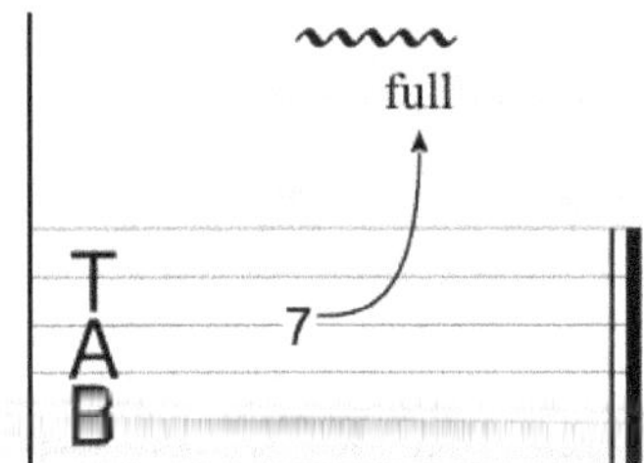

Bend release with vibrato.

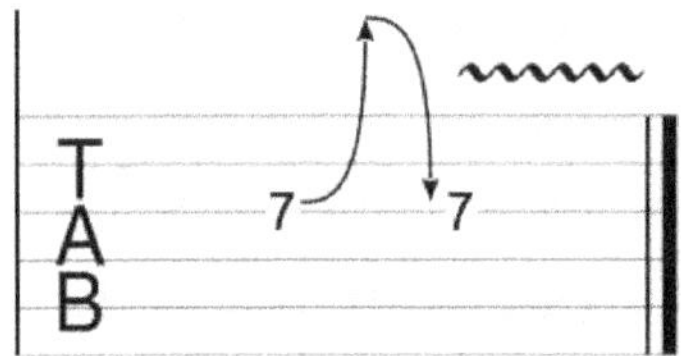

Just like before, you want to add these techniques together to get the most out of them.

By mastering slides, bends, and vibrato, you'll elevate your guitar playing to new levels of expressiveness and creativity. These techniques are essential for crafting solos that not only showcase technical skill but also connect emotionally with your audience, leaving a lasting impression.

Lesson 9: Double Stops and Harmonics

Guitarists seeking to expand their sonic palette and add depth to their playing can benefit significantly from mastering double stops and harmonics. These techniques offer unique tonal possibilities and are essential tools for creating rich, textured soundscapes.

Creating Thick Sounds with Double Stops

Double stops involve playing two notes simultaneously, producing a thicker, more complex sound. It can add a powerful dimension to solos and rhythm playing. Here's how to effectively use double stops:

1. **Basic Double Stops:** Start by playing two adjacent strings with one or two fingers. Experiment with different intervals, such as thirds and fifths, to explore various harmonic sounds.

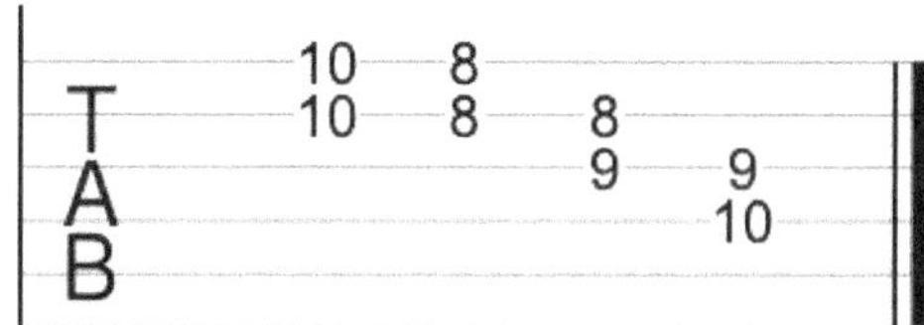

Example of double stops along the fretboard.

1. **Sliding Double Stops:** Incorporate slides into your double stops to create smooth, flowing transitions. This method adds expressiveness and movement to your playing.
2. **Rhythmic Patterns:** Use double stops in rhythmic patterns to add punch and excitement to your chords. This approach is particularly effective in rock and blues contexts.

Sliding into double stops within a rhythm pattern.

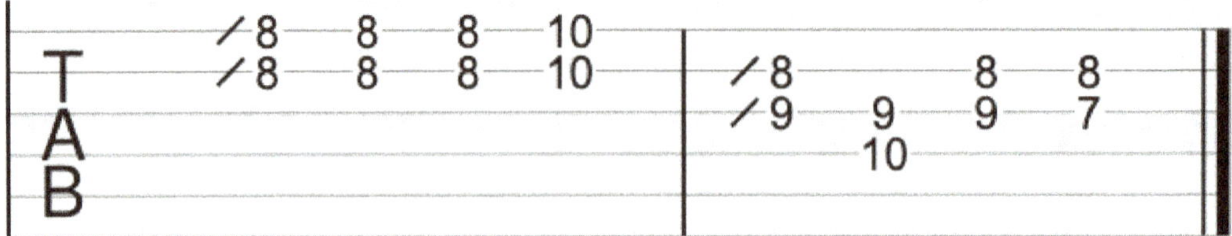

Double stops can be used in both rhythm and lead guitar playing. By mastering this technique, you can enhance your abilities in both of these areas of your guitar playing.

Utilizing Natural and Artificial Harmonics

Harmonics are an advanced technique that produces bell-like, ethereal tones by lightly touching the string at specific points. They can add shimmering accents and haunting melodies to your music. Here's how to master both natural and artificial harmonics:

1. **Natural Harmonics:**
    - Lightly touch the string directly above the fret wire at harmonic nodes such as the 5th, 7th, and 12th frets. Pluck the string to produce a clear harmonic tone.
    - Experiment with different positions to explore the range of sounds available through natural harmonics.
2. **Artificial Harmonics:**
    - Fret a note with one hand while lightly touching the string at a harmonic point with the picking hand. This technique allows you to play harmonics on any note, expanding your creative possibilities.
    - Practice precision and coordination to ensure clear, ringing tones when using artificial harmonics.

Both of these techniques can add dramatic flair as well as a precise way to tune your instrument by ear.

Natural Harmonics

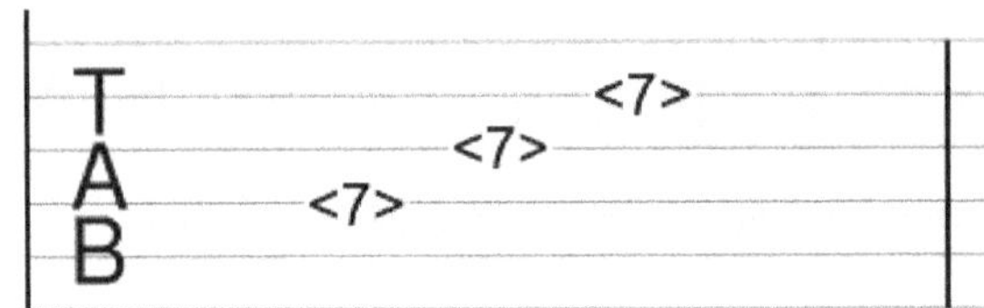

Artificial Harmonics

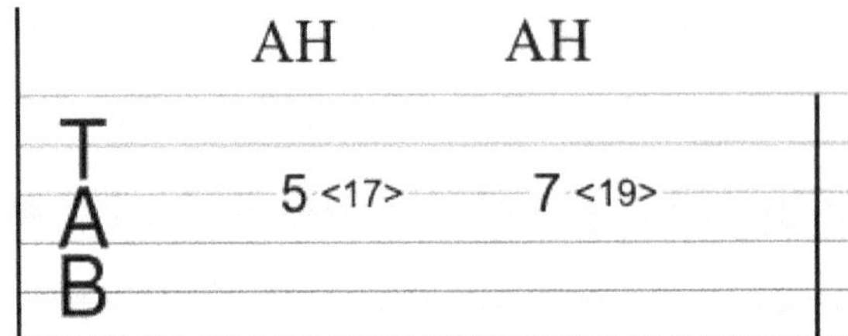

Natural harmonics are created by tapping on the fret wires on certain frets along the fretboard. Producing a bell-like effect. Artificial harmonics are created by rubbing your thumb slightly along the string after you pick it. Producing a squeal-type effect.

By incorporating double stops and harmonics into your repertoire, you'll enrich your guitar playing with layers of texture and sonic variety. These techniques will enhance your ability to create dynamic and captivating performances, whether you're crafting intricate solos or adding depth to rhythm sections.

Chapter III Quiz

In chapter 3, you have learned about soloing techniques. Such things as hammer-ons, pull-offs, bends, slides, etc. These are what allow you to bring the scales to life.

Q: What is the primary benefit of learning hammer-ons?
A: ____

Q: What technique complements the hammer-on?
A: ____

Q: What kind of effect do slides and bends produce?
A: ____

Q: How does vibrato affect a note played on the guitar?
A: ____

Q: What is the primary characteristic of double stops?
A: ____

Q: Which techniques produce bell and squealing-type tones?
A: ____

Chapter III summary

First, you learned about hammer-ons and pull-offs. These are fundamental guitar techniques in lead guitar playing. Enabling fluid motion with minimal picking.

Second, you learned techniques for mastering hammer-ons and pull-offs. As well as how to combine them for enhanced fluid musical phrases. Building speed and efficiency.

Third, we learn about slides, bends, and vibrato. Three fundamental techniques that give character to the notes when creating melodic phrasing. Mastering these elevates your guitar playing to new levels of creative expression.

Fourth, you then learned about double stops. These are where you play two notes simultaneously, producing a thicker, more complex tone. This technique can enhance both rhythm and lead guitar playing.

Lastly, you learned about harmonics. An excellent tool for creating bell-like sounds that can add shimmering accents and haunting melodies to your music. Allowing you to add layers of texture and sonic variety to your music.

Chapter IV: Improvisational Skills

Lesson 10: Developing Phrasing

Developing effective phrasing is a crucial aspect of becoming a skilled lead guitarist. Phrasing refers to the way you shape and structure your musical ideas, much like forming sentences in speech. Mastering this skill allows you to convey emotions more powerfully and connect with your audience on a deeper level.

Crafting Memorable Phrases

Creating memorable phrases involves more than just playing notes in sequence; it's about giving your music a voice and character. Here are some strategies to help you craft phrases that resonate with listeners:

- **Start with a Motif:** Begin with a simple musical idea or motif and build on it. Repeating and developing this motif can create familiarity and make your phrases more memorable.

- **Vary Your Articulation:** Experiment with different articulations, such as staccato, legato, and accents, to add texture and interest to your phrases. This variation keeps your audience engaged.
- **Use Space Effectively:** Silence is a powerful tool in music. Incorporate pauses and rests within your phrases to create tension and allow your music to breathe.

Using Dynamics for Impact

Dynamics, or the variation in loudness, play a significant role in making your guitar playing expressive and impactful. Here are some ways to use dynamics to enhance your phrasing:

- **Contrast Volume Levels:** Alternate between soft and loud passages to create contrast and emphasis. This technique can highlight specific notes or phrases, making them stand out.

This concept allows you to control the emotion of the message that you are trying to convey in your music.

- **Gradual Changes:** Employ crescendos (gradually increasing volume) and decrescendos (gradually decreasing volume) to add emotional depth to your playing. These dynamic shifts can lead to more compelling musical narratives.
- **Dynamic Accents:** Use sudden changes in dynamics to accentuate key moments in your solos, adding drama and excitement.

Creating a Dialogue

Phrasing can also be thought of as a musical dialogue, where each phrase responds to or complements the previous one. This conversational approach can make your playing more engaging and relatable:

- **Call and Response:** Use the call-and-response technique by playing a phrase and then following it with a complementary or contrasting phrase. This interaction can create a sense of conversation within your music.

This technique is widespread in blues and rock music. This can be done with two guitars, vocal and guitar, or other instruments.

- **Question and Answer:** Structure your phrases like a question and answer, where one phrase poses a musical question and the following words provide a resolution. This technique can add intrigue and keep listeners engaged.
- **Thematic Development:** Introduce a theme or motif and develop it throughout your solo. Repeating and varying this theme can create cohesion and a sense of storytelling within your music.

By focusing on expressing emotion through melody and creating a musical dialogue, you'll enhance your phrasing skills and deepen your connection with your audience. These techniques will enable you to craft more compelling and expressive solos, elevating your overall guitar playing.

By crafting memorable phrases and using dynamics effectively, you'll develop a unique and expressive voice on the guitar. These skills are essential for captivating your audience and elevating your musical storytelling.

Lesson 11: Alternate and Tremolo Picking

Alternate and tremolo picking are essential techniques for any guitarist aspiring to play with speed, precision, and expression. Mastering these picking styles will enable you to execute fast runs.

Understanding Alternate Picking

Alternate picking involves using a consistent pattern of downstrokes and upstrokes to pluck the strings.

- **Basic Technique:** Begin by holding your pick correctly, using a relaxed grip. Practice alternating between downstrokes and upstrokes on a single string, aiming for an even and controlled motion.

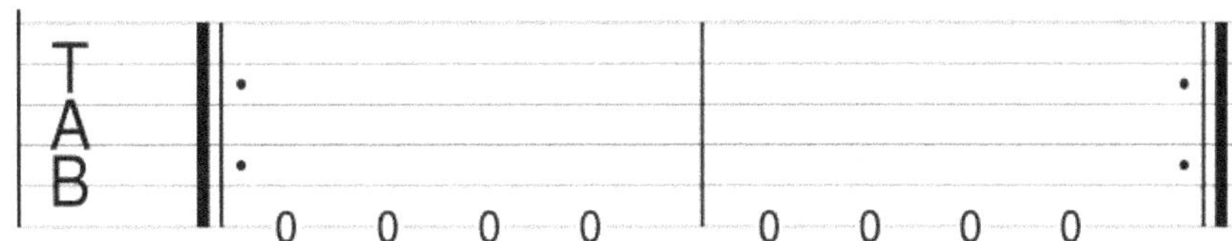

Pick each note alternatively. First one down, second one up, third one down, and the fourth one back up, etc.

- **Economy of Motion:** Keep your picking hand close to the strings to minimize unnecessary movement. This economy of motion enables faster, more accurate play.
- **Consistent Timing:** Use a metronome to maintain a steady tempo. Start slowly to ensure accuracy, then gradually increase speed as you become more comfortable with the alternate-picking motion.
- **Application Across Strings:** Once you're comfortable with alternate picking on a single string, practice transitioning smoothly between strings. This skill is crucial for playing scales and arpeggios fluidly.

Economy of motion, consistent timing, and application across strings all contribute to acquiring control with the pick to execute fast, fluid movements. These concepts should be practiced daily.

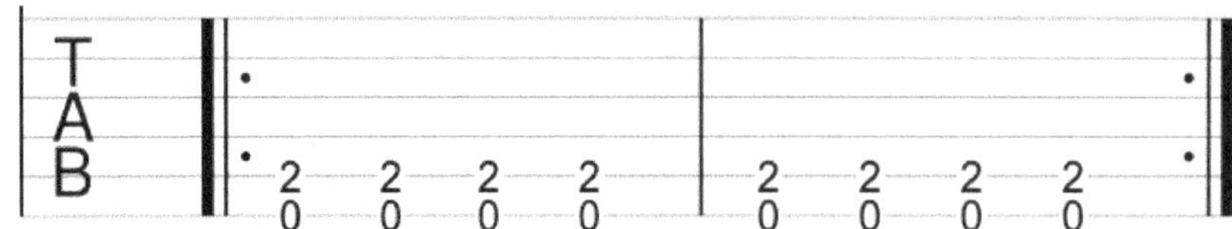

This is done with the open E chord. Listen to how it sounds when playing it like this.

- **Basic Technique:** Similar to alternate picking, tremolo picking involves playing at twice the speed with a relaxed grip and controlled motion. Focus on maintaining a steady rhythm and even volume between strokes.

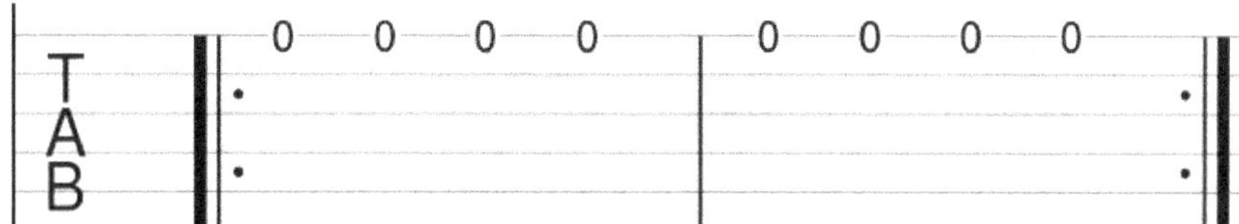

In this example, do the same thing as before, but on the 1st string. Use an up-down motion on each note, but this time, twice as fast. This is the essence of shred guitar.

- **Speed and Endurance:** Develop speed and endurance by practicing tremolo picking for extended periods. Start at a moderate pace and gradually increase the tempo, ensuring clarity and consistency.
- **Dynamic Control:** Experiment with different dynamic levels by adjusting the intensity of your picking. This control allows you to add emotional depth and variation to your playing.

Make sure to keep your picking hand close to the guitar body.

- **Musical Application:** Use tremolo picking to add tension and excitement to your solos. Incorporate it into your improvisation to create climactic moments and enhance the overall impact of your music.

Integrating Techniques into Your Playing

By mastering alternate and tremolo picking, you'll expand your technical repertoire and versatility as a guitarist. Here's how to integrate these techniques effectively:

- **Practice Exercises:** Incorporate alternate- and tremolo-picking exercises into your daily practice routine. Focus on accuracy, speed, and consistency to build proficiency over time.

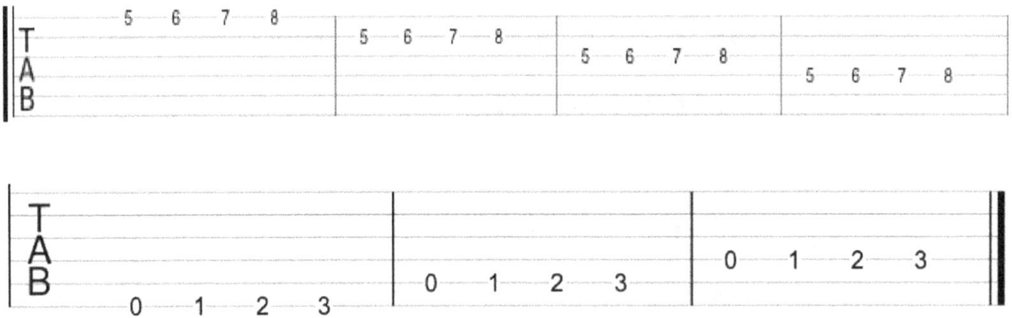

Practice these exercises daily with alternate and tremolo picking. Work with a metronome to enhance your accuracy.

- **Apply in Musical Contexts:** Use these techniques within musical pieces to bring your playing to life. Whether you're tackling a challenging riff or crafting an expressive solo, alternate and tremolo picking can add complexity and excitement.

Pull-offs, Slides, Hammer-ons, and Vibrato

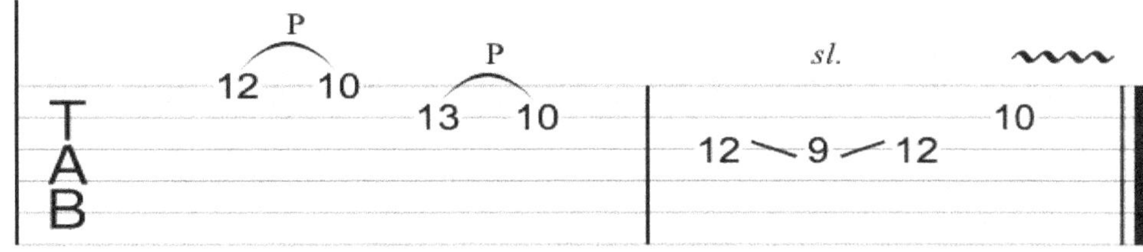

Pull-offs, Slides, and Vibrato.

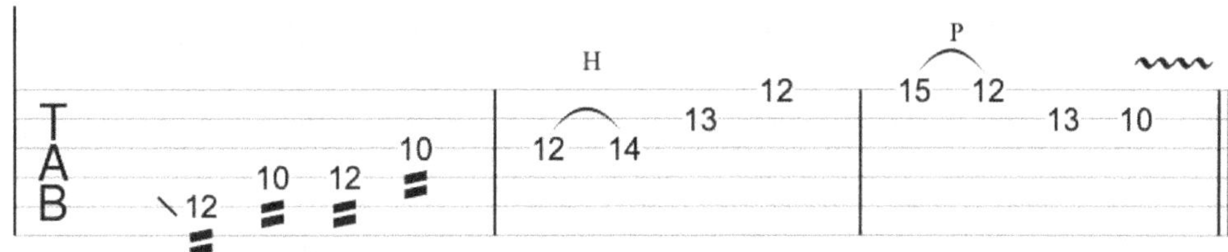

Tremolo Picking, Hammer-on, Pull-off, and Vibrato.

Practice these types of techniques daily in a musical context.

- **Explore Different Genres:** Experiment with these picking styles across various musical genres. From rock and metal to classical and jazz, alternate and tremolo picking can enhance your ability to adapt and innovate.

- **Seek Feedback:** Regularly seek constructive feedback from teachers, peers, or mentors to gain new insights and perspectives on your playing, helping you refine your technique and musical expression.

By exploring different genres, you expand your knowledge and creative use of these techniques, as each player uniquely approaches the guitar.

When you seek feedback, you avoid costly mistakes, and you not only gain insight into your own playing, but also the personal experiences of others you didn't think of.

By focusing on alternate and tremolo picking, you'll gain the skills to play with greater speed, precision, and expression. These techniques are essential for any guitarist striving to elevate their playing and create dynamic, engaging performances.

Lesson 12: Crafting a Memorable Solo

Crafting a memorable solo is an art that combines technical skill, creativity, and emotional expression. A great solo not only showcases your proficiency as a guitarist but also tells a story that resonates with your audience.

So let's explore key elements and techniques to help you create solos that leave a lasting impression. Just like an artist does with a painting, and an author does with a book.

Understanding Solo Structure

A well-structured solo provides a clear beginning, middle, and end, guiding the listener through a musical journey. Here's how to construct a compelling solo:

- **Introduction:** Start with a strong opening phrase that captures attention. This could be a bold riff or a melodic motif that sets the tone for your solo.

Listen to your favorite songs and analyze what technique catches your attention and pulls you in.

- **Development:** Build on your initial idea by introducing variations and exploring different scales or techniques. This section should create momentum and maintain the listener's interest.
- **Climax:** Reach a peak moment in your solo with a high-energy phrase or an emotional bend. This is where you can showcase your technical prowess and creativity.
- **Resolution:** Conclude your solo by resolving tension and returning to the central theme or motif. A well-crafted ending leaves a satisfying impression on the listener.

Techniques for Emotional Impact

To create solos that resonate emotionally, consider incorporating the following techniques.

- **Dynamics:** Use variations in volume and intensity to convey emotion. Softer passages can evoke introspection, while louder sections add excitement and passion.

Dynamics allow you to create contrast, build tension, shape phrases, and lead the listener on a journey through intimate, memorable musical landscapes.

- **Phrasing:** Shape your musical ideas with thoughtful phrasing. Use pauses, accents, and articulation to add character and expressiveness to your playing.
- **Vibrato and Bends:** These techniques add a vocal quality to your playing, allowing you to express emotion more deeply. Use vibrato to sustain notes with warmth, and bends to create tension and release.
- **Melodic Development:** Craft melodies that are memorable and singable. Focus on creating phrases that tell a story and connect with the listener on an emotional level.

Incorporating Creativity

Infuse your solos with creativity by exploring new ideas and techniques:

- **Scale Variations:** Experiment with different scales and modes to add color and complexity to your solos. The pentatonic scale is a great starting point, but don't hesitate to incorporate the blues scale, major scale, or modes like Dorian or Mixolydian.

The Major Scale: 1 2 3 4 5 6 7

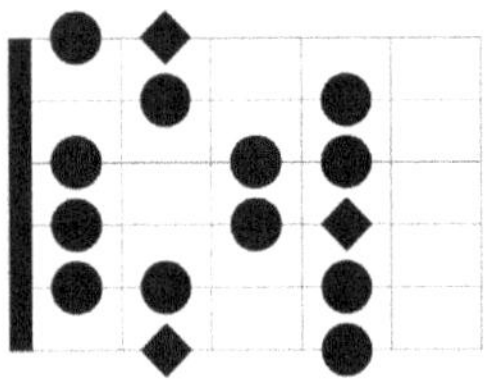

This is the foundation of all scales.

The Minor Blues Scale: 1 b3 4 b5 5 6 b7

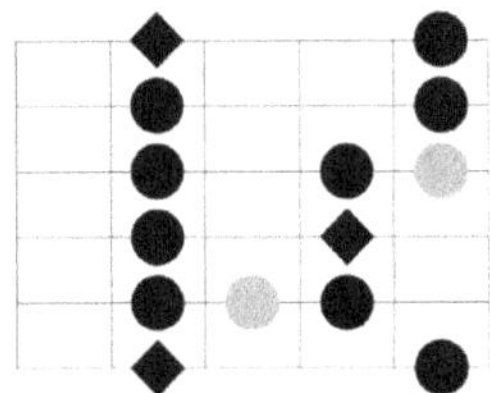

The minor pentatonic scale with the "blue" note.

The Dorian Mode: 1 2 b3 4 5 6 b7

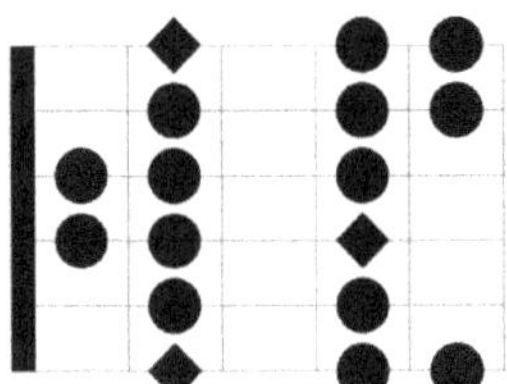

This is the 2nd mode of the major scale.

The Mixolydian Mode: 1 2 3 4 5 6 b7

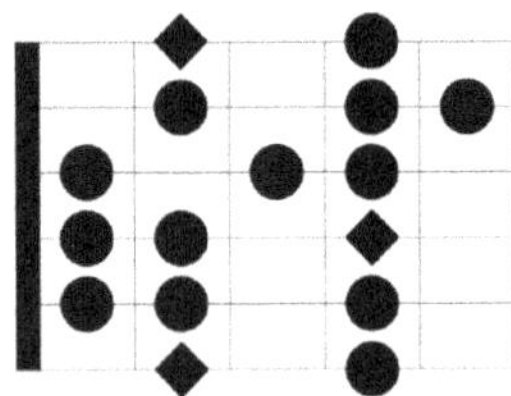

This is the 5th mode of the major scale.

All these scales and more like them can be used to craft memorable solos. The goal is to know the note formula.

- **Rhythmic Diversity:** Vary your rhythms to keep your solos interesting. Incorporate syncopation, triplets, or odd time signatures to add a unique twist.
- **Improvisation:** Allow room for spontaneity in your solos. Improvisation can lead to unexpected and innovative ideas that enhance the overall musical experience.

Practice and Refinement

To craft memorable solos, consistent practice and refinement are essential:

- **Record and Analyze:** Regularly record your solos, then listen back to identify your strengths and areas for improvement. This self-assessment helps you refine your technique and creativity.
- **Seek Inspiration:** Listen to solos from your favorite guitarists and analyze what makes them effective. Draw inspiration from different genres and styles to expand your musical vocabulary.

- **Experiment and Iterate:** Don't be afraid to experiment with new ideas and techniques. Iteration is key to developing a unique style that reflects your musical personality.

- **Experiment with Different Styles:** Explore various musical genres and styles to expand your versatility as a guitarist. This exploration can introduce you to new techniques and inspire creative approaches to your playing.

By focusing on structure, emotional impact, creativity, and consistent practice, you'll be able to craft solos that captivate and resonate with your audience.

These skills will enhance your ability to express yourself through music and leave a lasting impression with every performance.

Chapter IV Quiz

In Chapter 4, you have learned about improvisational skills.
These are what's needed for effective lead guitar playing.
Phrasing, alternate picking, and crafting memorable solos.

Q: What is a key strategy for crafting memorable phrasing?

A: ____

Q: How can dynamics enhance your guitar phrasing?

A: ____

Q: What is the primary benefit of mastering alternate picking?

A: ____

Q: What is a crucial aspect of tremolo picking?

A: ____

Q: What is an essential aspect of structuring a guitar solo?

A: ____

Q: How can you incorporate creativity into your guitar solos?

A: ____

Chapter IV Summary

<u>First</u>, you learn that developing effective phrasing is a crucial element of becoming a proficient lead guitarist. This refers to the way you shape and structure your musical ideas.

<u>Second</u>, you must remember that creating memorable phrasing involves more than just playing notes in sequence; it's about giving your solos a musical voice and appealing character.

<u>Third</u>, you learn that one way of doing this is through alternate and tremolo picking. These are two ways to master expression through speed and precision.

<u>Fourth</u>, economy of motion, consistent timing, and application across all strings contribute to control with the pick. Allowing you to execute fast, fluid movements and excel in dynamic, expressive performances.

<u>Lastly</u>, you learned how to craft a memorable solo and how all these things can contribute. Focus on structure, creativity, emotional impact, and consistent practice to create engaging solos that captivate and resonate with your audience.

Chapter V: Style Exploration

Lesson 13: Blues Influence

The blues has been a profound influence on modern music, shaping genres such as rock and pop. Understanding and incorporating blues elements into your guitar playing can add depth and emotion. This gives your music a timeless quality.

Blues licks are short, expressive phrases that capture the essence of the blues sound. These licks are characterized by their use of the minor pentatonic scale, expressive bends, and soulful articulation.

Here's how to effectively integrate blues licks into your playing:

1. **Learn Classic Licks:** Start by learning iconic blues licks from influential guitarists such as B.B. King, Muddy Waters, and Stevie Ray Vaughan. These licks provide a foundation for understanding the blues language.

Classic Blues Licks

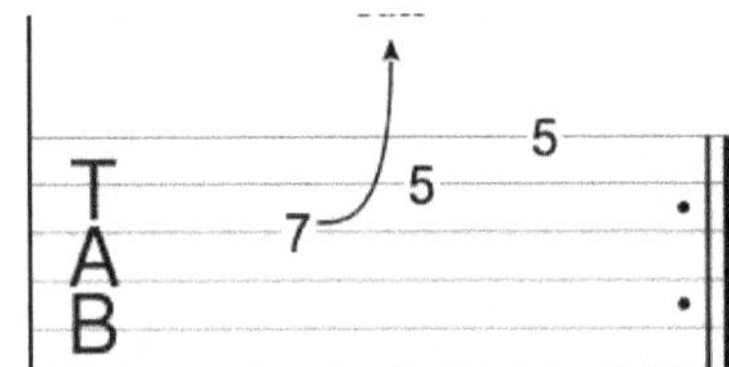

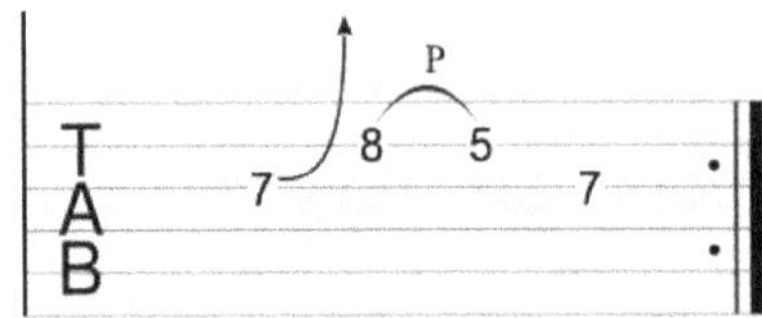

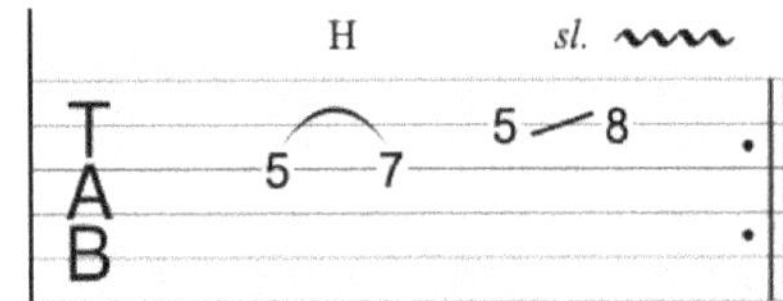

These are standard blues licks found in many guitar solos from your favorite artists.

Focus on Feel and Emotion

Blue's licks are not just about the notes but also about the emotion conveyed. Pay attention to the nuances, such as bends, slides, and vibrato, which add expressiveness to your licks.

Understanding Blues Progressions

The 12-bar blues progression is a fundamental structure in blues music, providing a framework for improvisation and composition.

1. **Basic 12-Bar Structure:** The classic 12-bar blues progression typically consists of three chords: I, IV, and V. In the key of E, these would be E7, A7, and B7. The progression follows a specific pattern over twelve measures.

There are hundreds, if not thousands, of songs that utilize the 12-bar blues progression. A great way to get started with chord progressions.

This progression is created with three chords played over 12 bars of music. The reason this is so popular is that once recognized, you can tell where it is going before it gets there.

Let's take a look at this in more detail.

The 12-Bar Blues Progression

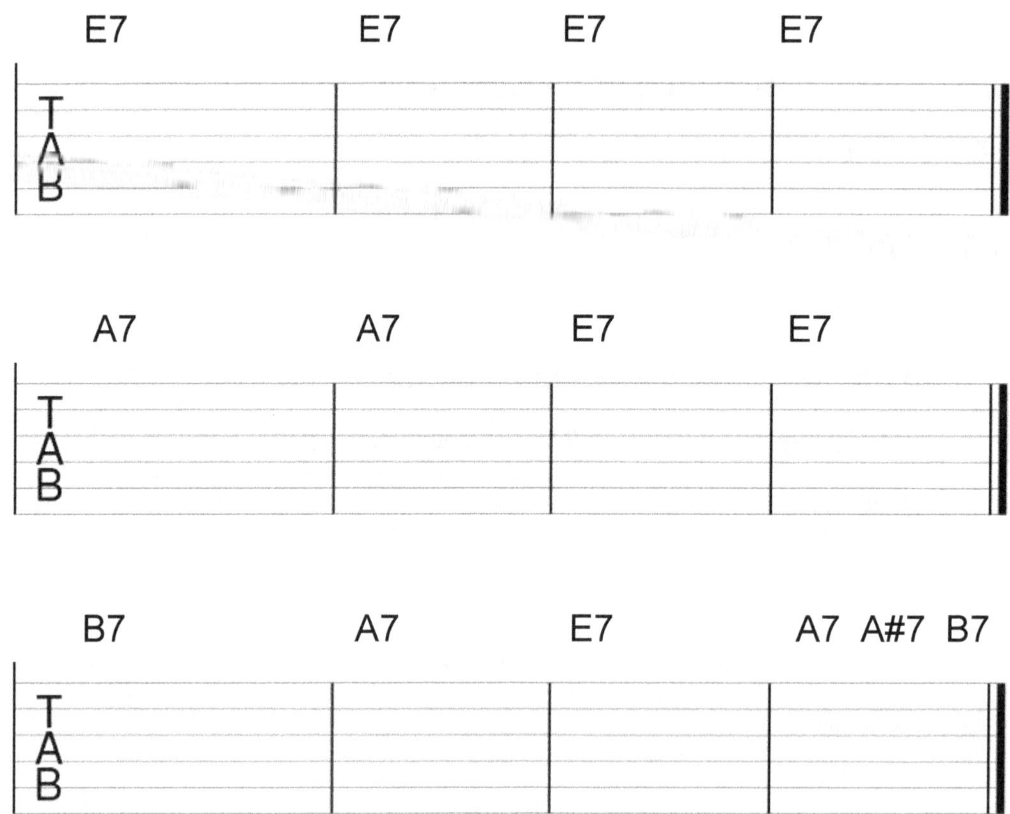

By mastering blues licks and progressions, you'll gain a deeper appreciation for the blues and its influence on modern music. These skills will enhance your ability to express emotion and creativity in your guitar playing, whether you're crafting solos or composing your own music.

Lesson 14: Rock Essentials

Rock music has long been a staple of popular culture, characterized by its powerful sound, driving rhythms, and rebellious spirit. This lesson will delve into the essential elements of rock guitar playing, helping you to capture the energy and attitude that define this genre.

Classic rock is built on iconic riffs that have stood the test of time. Mastering these riffs is key to understanding the foundation of rock music and developing your own style.

Classic Rock Riffs

Classic rock is built on iconic riffs that have stood the test of time. Mastering these riffs is key to understanding the foundation of rock music and developing your own style.

These are the backbone of the genre, characterized by their memorable melodies and powerful chord progressions. They often rely on power chords and catchy hooks, making them instantly recognizable and enduringly popular.

1. **Learn Iconic Riffs:** Start by learning riffs from legendary bands such as Led Zeppelin, AC/DC, and The Rolling Stones. These riffs highlight the use of power chords, palm muting, and syncopated rhythms, all of which are central to rock music.

2. **Focus on Timing and Precision:** Rock riffs often feature tight, precise playing. Practice with a metronome to ensure your timing is spot-on and your rhythm is consistent.

3. **Experiment with Variations:** Once you're comfortable with the basic riffs, experiment with variations by adding embellishments like slides, bends, and hammer-ons to make the riffs your own.

By engaging in these three concepts, you learn to build rock guitar riffs of your own. Learn rock riffs from your favorite players, focus on their timing and rhythm, and learn to craft great guitar riffs of your own.

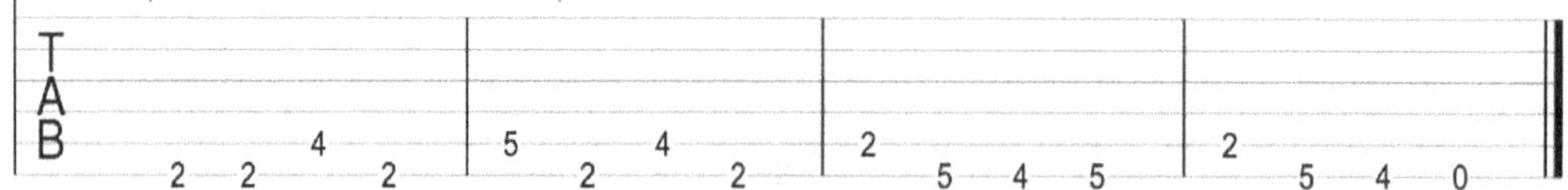

Here is an example of a popular guitar riff. As you can see, it uses single notes over two strings.

Energy and Attitude in Rock

Rock music is not just about the notes you play; it's about the energy and attitude you bring to your performance. Here are some strategies to infuse your playing with the essence of rock:

- **Embrace Power Chords:** Power chords are the backbone of rock music, providing a strong, punchy sound. Practice shifting between power chords smoothly to create a driving, energetic feel.

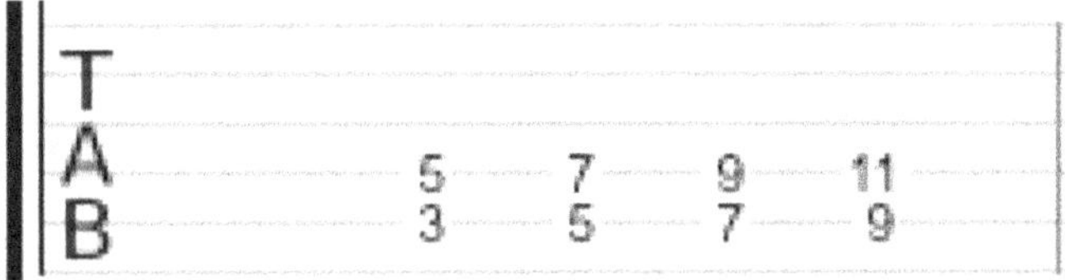

These types of chords are simple two-note structures that have a lot of power when played loudly with distortion, the most common type of guitar chord in rock and heavy metal.

Make sure to master playing power chords, as these can allow you to easily move up and down the fretboard without changing your chord shape. With regular open chords, you change shape. With power chords, you don't.

- **Amplify Your Sound:** Experiment with different amplification settings to achieve a powerful tone. Adding distortion or overdrive can enhance the raw energy of your playing.
- **Exude Confidence:** Rock is all about attitude. Play with confidence and conviction, using stage presence and body language to communicate the rebellious spirit of rock music.

Rock guitar is an exciting form of music because it lets you go beyond just plugging into a guitar amplifier. It encourages creativity by using alternative amp settings (increasing gain), guitar pedals, and effects processors to enhance your musical landscapes.

By mastering classic rock riffs and embodying the energy and attitude of rock, you'll be able to create powerful and engaging performances. These skills will not only enhance your technical abilities but also allow you to connect with the essence of rock music.

Lesson 15: Mastering Phrasing

Mastering phrasing and improvisation is crucial for any guitarist looking to create memorable solos and express their unique musical voice. This lesson will explore advanced techniques that will enhance your ability to craft engaging phrases and improvise with confidence.

Phrasing Techniques

Phrasing is the art of shaping musical ideas into coherent and expressive statements. It involves more than just playing notes; it's about giving your music a voice and character.

- **Motif Development:** Begin with a simple motif or theme. Develop this idea by varying its rhythm, melody, or harmony. Repetition with subtle changes can make your music memorable while maintaining interest.

- **Use of Space:** Silence can be as powerful as sound. Incorporate pauses and rests to create tension and allow your music to breathe. Strategic use of space can make your phrases more dynamic and impactful.
- **Articulation Variety:** Experiment with different articulations such as staccato, legato, and accents. These variations can add texture and nuance to your playing, making your phrases more expressive.

Exploring Improvisation

Improvisation is the ability to create and perform music spontaneously. It requires a deep understanding of musical theory and a strong sense of creativity.

- **Scale Proficiency:** Familiarize yourself with various scales, especially the pentatonic, blues, and major/minor scales. Being comfortable with these scales allows you to navigate the fretboard effortlessly during improvisation.

Remember, these are the foundations of music. Knowledge of scales will enhance your abilities to craft rhythms and solos.

Scales For Crafting Rhythms and Solos

The Major Scale

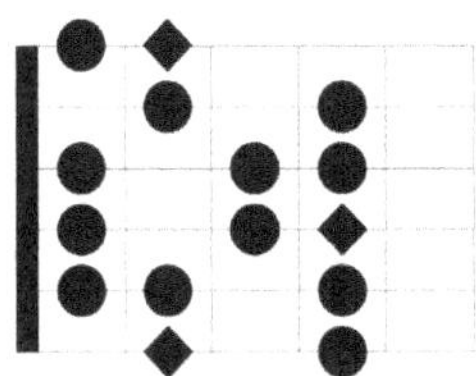

Known for its happy, uplifting sound.

The Minor Scale

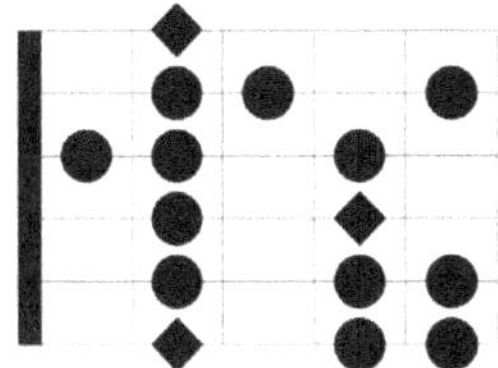

Known for its sad, somber sound.

The Minor Pentatonic Scale

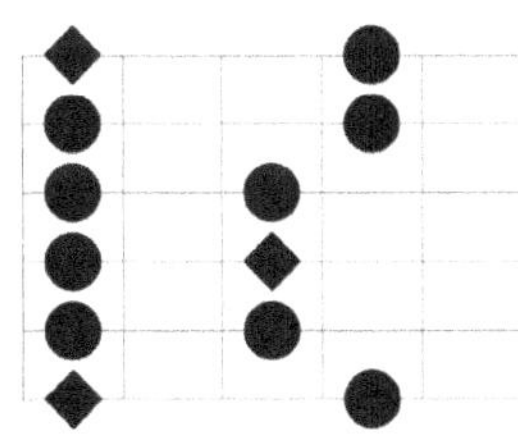

A simpler version of the minor scale.

The Minor Bues Scale

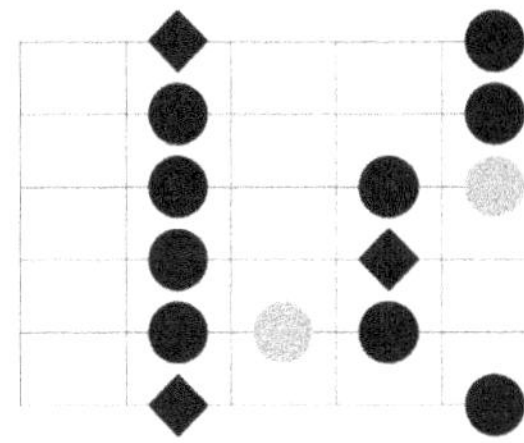

An extension of the minor pentatonic scale.

Use these scales as the foundation of your guitar playing prowess. Know them well, and they will allow you to unlock the mysteries of the fretboard.

- **Rhythmic Exploration:** Experiment with different rhythmic patterns and syncopations Changing the rhythm can transform a simple phrase into something exciting and fresh.

- **Dynamic Expression:** Utilize dynamics to convey emotion. Play with variations in volume and intensity to add depth and drama to your improvisation.

- **Listening and Interaction:** When improvising with others, listen closely to what they are playing. Respond to their musical cues to create a musical conversation. This interaction can lead to innovative and unexpected musical moments.

By refining your phrasing techniques and exploring new avenues in improvisation, you'll be able to craft solos that are both technically proficient and deeply expressive. These skills will empower you to leave a lasting impression on your audience and elevate your overall musicianship.

Chapter V Quiz

In chapter five, you learned about style exploration. Styles such as blues, rock, and phrasing mastery. All things that will expand your musical landscape.

Q: How do blues licks add expressiveness to your solo?
A: ____

Q: What blues structures provide a framework for improvising?
A: ____

Q: Why is playing rock riffs essential in rock music?
A: ____

Q: What features contribute to rock music's energetic feel
A: ____

Q: What phrasing technique creates dynamics in soloing?
A: ____

Q: How does improvisation contribute to creating solos?
A: ____

Chapter V Summary

<u>First,</u> you learn how the blues has influenced modern music, shaping styles such as rock and pop. Adding these types of elements to your playing can add depth and emotion to your guitar soloing landscapes

<u>Second</u>, you learn that one of the best ways to do this is to study classic blues licks. These are phrases that convey emotional content and add more expression to your solos.

<u>Third</u>, you learn about rock essentials. These concepts and techniques help you expand your musical creativity and inspiration, starting with guitar riffs and driving rhythms.

<u>Fourth</u>, rock music isn't just about the notes you express through your playing; it's taken a step further by adding attitude and over-the-top energy that entices the audience not just to listen, but to take action.

<u>Lastly</u>, by refining your improvisational techniques, adding energy and attitude, you'll develop skills that empower you. These will leave a lasting impression on your audience and elevate your overall musicianship.

Chapter VI: Creative Expression

Lesson 16: Melodic Creativity

Exploring melodic creativity is essential for any guitarist looking to develop a unique musical voice. This lesson will guide you through techniques for crafting distinctive melodies and using the pentatonic scale in innovative ways, transforming your guitar playing into a personal and expressive art form.

Crafting Unique Melodies

Creating memorable melodies involves more than just stringing together notes. It requires an understanding of musical structure, emotion, and rhythm. Here are some strategies to help you craft unique melodies:

- **Start with a Simple Idea:** Begin with a basic musical motif or idea. This could be a short sequence of notes or a rhythmic pattern. Simplicity allows you to focus on developing the concept into something more complex.

- **Experiment with Intervals.** Vary the intervals between notes to create unexpected and interesting melodies. Larger intervals can add drama and tension, while smaller ones can develop a sense of fluidity and continuity.
- **Incorporate Dynamics:** Use variations in volume and intensity to shape your melody. Dynamics can transform a simple line into an emotionally powerful statement.
- **Play with Rhythms:** Experiment with different rhythmic patterns and syncopations. Changing the rhythm can breathe new life into a melody, making it more engaging.

Using the Pentatonic Scale Creatively

The pentatonic scale is a versatile tool that can be used creatively to generate fresh and exciting musical ideas. Here's how you can go beyond the basics and explore its full potential:

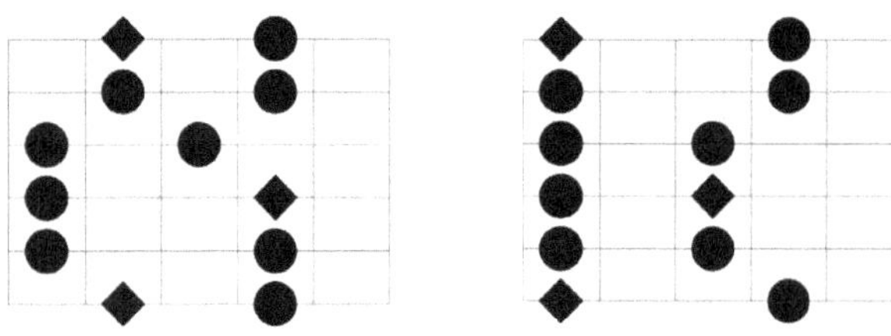

Major Pentatonic   Minor Pentatonic

*Make sure to master these two scale patterns.

- **Explore Different Positions:** Familiarize yourself with all five positions of the pentatonic scale on the fretboard. Shifting between these positions can open up new melodic possibilities and facilitate smoother transitions.
- **Blend with Other Scales:** Combine the pentatonic scale with other scales, such as the blues scale or the major scale, to add complexity and richness to your melodies. This blending can lead to innovative and unexpected musical results.
- **Use Passing Tones:** Incorporate passing tones—notes that aren't part of the pentatonic scale—to add tension and color to your phrases. These tones can create a sense of movement and direction in your melodies.
- **Experiment with Techniques:** Apply techniques like bends, slides, and hammer-ons to the pentatonic scale. These techniques can add expressiveness and flair, making your melodies more dynamic and personal.

These techniques can add expressiveness and flair, making your melodies more dynamic and personal.

Different Positions: (additional pentatonic patterns)

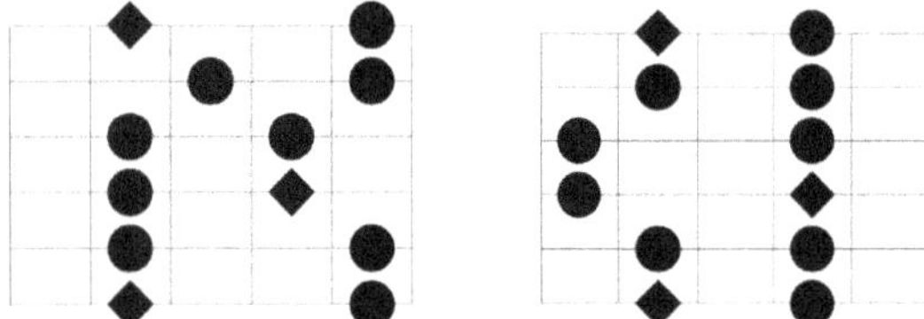

Other scales To Blend With: (harmonic and melodic minor)

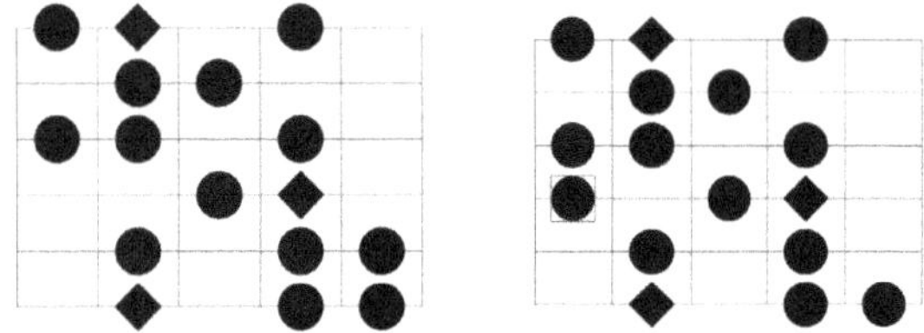

Passing Tones: (minor and major blues)

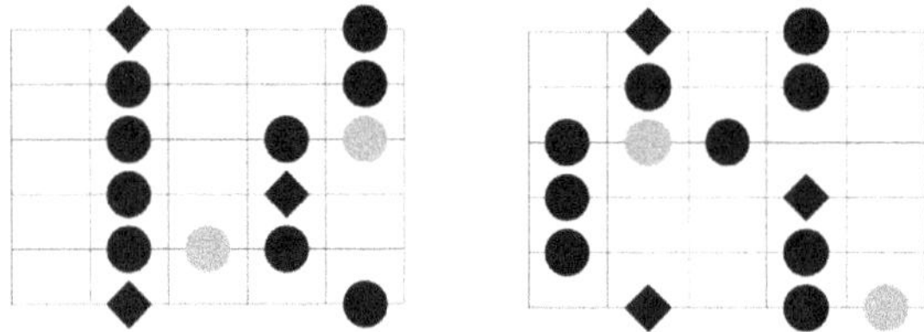

By focusing on crafting unique melodies and using the pentatonic scale creatively, you'll develop a distinctive musical style that sets you apart as a guitarist. These skills will enable you to express your artistic vision and connect more deeply with listeners.

Lesson 17: Emotional Connection

Connecting emotionally through your guitar playing is a crucial aspect of musical expression. It's the difference between playing notes accurately and truly moving an audience. In this lesson, we'll explore how to convey emotions through your guitar and create a deep connection with your listeners.

Expressing Emotion through Guitar

The guitar is a versatile instrument capable of expressing a wide range of emotions. Here are some techniques to help you convey emotion more effectively:

- **Dynamic Range:** Use variations in volume to express different emotions. Softer passages can convey intimacy and tenderness, while louder sections can evoke passion and excitement. Experiment with crescendos and decrescendos to add emotional depth.

- **Phrasing and Timing:** The way you phrase your notes and manage timing can significantly affect the emotional impact of your playing. Allow your music to breathe by incorporating pauses and varying your note lengths. This can create tension and release, much like a conversation.

- **Vibrato and Bends:** These techniques add a human-like quality to your playing, allowing you to mimic the expressive nuances of the human voice. Use vibrato to add warmth and emotion to sustained notes, while bends can inject a sense of yearning or intensity.

- **Choice of Scales and Modes:** Different scales can evoke different moods. For example, the minor pentatonic scale often conveys a more melancholic feel, while major scales can sound uplifting and joyful. Experiment with various scales to find the ones that best express your intended emotion.

Connecting with Your Audience

To create a lasting emotional impact, it's essential to connect with your audience on a personal level. Here are some strategies to enhance this connection:

- **Intentional Performance:** Approach each performance with a clear emotional intent. Consider what you want your audience to feel and tailor your playing to evoke that response. This intention will guide your musical choices.
- **Engagement:** Make eye contact with your audience and use body language to convey enthusiasm and passion. Your physical presence can reinforce the emotions you're expressing through your music.
- **Storytelling:** Use your music to tell a story. Whether through lyrics, melodies, or the structure of your piece, aim to take your audience on a journey. This narrative approach helps listeners connect with your music on a deeper level.
- **Authenticity:** Be genuine in your expression. Audiences can sense when a performance is authentic, and this authenticity can create a powerful emotional connection.

By focusing on emotional expression and audience connection, you'll enhance your ability to move listeners and create memorable musical experiences. These skills are fundamental for any guitarist seeking to transcend technical proficiency and achieve true artistic expression.

Lesson 18: Storytelling with Music

Storytelling is a powerful tool that transcends language and culture, allowing musicians to convey emotions, experiences, and narratives through their instruments. As a guitarist, learning to tell a story through your music can elevate your playing and create a profound connection with your audience.

Narrative Techniques in Solos

Crafting a solo with a narrative arc can transform it from a series of notes into an expressive tale that captivates listeners. Here are some techniques to help you weave storytelling into your solos:

- **Establish a Theme:** Start with a clear musical theme or motif that serves as the foundation of your story. This theme can be revisited and developed throughout the solo, providing cohesion and familiarity.

- **Develop Characters:** Introduce contrasting musical ideas or "characters" within your solo. Different melodic lines, rhythms, or dynamics can represent these. The interaction between these characters can add depth and complexity to your narrative.

- **Build Tension and Release:** Create tension through dissonant notes, faster rhythms, or dynamic crescendos. This tension can culminate in a climactic moment, followed by a resolution that offers release and satisfaction to the listener.

- **Use Dynamics and Tempo Changes:** Vary the volume and speed to reflect different parts of your story. Sudden changes can signify shifts in mood or plot, while gradual variations can enhance the overall emotional journey.

Creating Compelling Musical Journeys

A compelling musical journey takes the audience on an emotional ride, leaving a lasting impression. Here's how you can craft such journeys through your guitar playing:

- **Start with a Strong Opening.** Capture your audience's attention from the very beginning with a bold and memorable opening phrase.

- **Explore Emotional Peaks and Valleys:** Guide your audience through a range of emotions by varying the intensity and mood of your music. Balance moments of high energy with softer, introspective passages to keep the journey engaging.

- **Incorporate Repetition and Variation:** Use repetition to reinforce key musical ideas, but introduce variations to maintain interest. This technique mirrors storytelling.

- **Conclude with a Satisfying Ending:** Bring your musical journey to a strong close that resolves the narrative. This could be a return to the initial theme or an unexpected twist that leaves the audience with something to ponder.

By mastering the art of storytelling with music, you'll enrich your guitar playing with compelling narratives that resonate with listeners. These skills will enable you to create memorable performances that not only showcase your technical abilities but also touch your audience's hearts and minds.

Chapter VI Quiz

In chapter six, you have learned about creative ways to express yourself more coherently. With melodic creativity, emotional connection, and storytelling in your music.

Q: What is an excellent strategy for crafting unique melodies?
A: ____

Q: How can the pentatonic scale be used creatively in a solo?
A: ____

Q: What is a technique used to express emotion in a solo?
A: ____

Q: How do you create a deeper connection in a performance?
A: ____

Q: What is an effective way to create a narrative in your solo?
A: ____

Q: What role does dynamics play in storytelling in music?
A: ____

Chapter VI Summary

<u>First</u>, you learn that exploring melodic creativity is essential for any guitarist looking to develop a unique musical voice, and in contract, using the pentatonic scales in innovative ways

<u>Second</u>, you learn that combining the pentatonic scale with other scales, such as the major or natural minor, can add complexity and richness to your melodies.

<u>Third</u>, you learn that knowing how to connect emotionally is a crucial aspect of musical expression. The guitar is a perfect instrument for expressing passion and excitement.

<u>Fourth</u>, you learn that the objective is to create a compelling story. Storytelling through your guitar playing can elevate your performance and help you make a profound connection with your audience.

<u>Lastly</u>, you learn that mastering the art of storytelling with your music develops the skill of creating memorable performances that not only showcase your technical prowess but also touch your audience's hearts and minds.

Chapter VII: Performance Preparation

Lesson 19: Stage Presence

Developing a strong stage presence is crucial for any performer looking to captivate and engage an audience. It's not just about playing your instrument well; it's about how you present yourself and connect with those watching. A compelling stage presence can elevate a performance, making it memorable and impactful.

Confidence on Stage

Confidence is key to delivering a convincing performance. Here are some strategies to help build and project confidence on stage:

- Preparation is Key: Thoroughly rehearse your set to ensure you feel comfortable with the material. Knowing your parts inside and out will allow you to focus on your performance rather than worrying about mistakes.

- **Body Language:** Use open and expressive body language to convey confidence. Stand tall, make eye contact with the audience, and avoid fidgeting, which can distract from your performance.
- **Engage with the Music:** Let your passion for the music shine through. Move naturally to the rhythm and allow yourself to feel the music's emotions. This genuine engagement can be contagious, drawing the audience into your performance.

Engaging with the Audience

Connecting with your audience is essential for creating a memorable experience. Here are some ways to engage effectively:

- **Acknowledge the Audience:** Greet your audience warmly and thank them for being there. This simple gesture can make them feel appreciated and more connected to you.

- **Interactive Elements:** Incorporate moments in your performance that allow you to interact with the audience, such as call-and-response sections or asking them to clap along. This interaction can create a sense of community and involvement.
- **Personal Stories:** Share brief anecdotes or insights about the songs you're performing. This personal touch can give context to your music and make your performance more relatable.
- **Respond to the Energy:** Pay attention to the audience's reactions and adjust your performance accordingly. If they're responding well to a particular song or style, consider extending that section or adding similar elements.

By cultivating confidence and engaging with your audience, you will enhance your stage presence and create performances that resonate long after the music ends. These skills are vital for any performer aiming to leave a lasting impression and build a loyal fanbase.

.

Lesson 20: Overcoming Nerves

Performing live can be an exhilarating experience, but it can also be accompanied by nervousness and anxiety. These feelings are entirely normal, even for seasoned musicians. Learning to manage performance anxiety effectively can help you deliver your best on stage and enjoy the experience more fully.

Techniques to Stay Calm

Managing nerves begins with developing strategies to stay calm both before and during your performance. Here are some techniques to help you maintain composure:

- **Deep Breathing:** Practice deep breathing exercises to help calm your mind and body. Take slow, deep breaths, inhaling through your nose and exhaling through your mouth. This can reduce tension and slow your heart rate.

- **Visualization:** Spend time visualizing a successful performance. Imagine yourself on stage, playing confidently and receiving positive reactions from the audience.
- **Mindfulness:** Engage in mindfulness practices to stay present and focused. Techniques such as meditation or yoga can help you develop a sense of calm and concentration, making it easier to manage nerves.
- **Warm-Up Routine:** Establish a consistent warm-up routine before going on stage. This not only prepares your fingers and voice but also serves as a comforting ritual that signals your body that it's time to perform.
- **Positive Affirmations:** Use positive affirmations to boost your confidence. Remind yourself of your strengths and past successes. Phrases like "I am prepared" or "I am capable" can reinforce a positive mindset.

Transforming Anxiety into Excitement

It's possible to reframe the energy of nerves into excitement, channeling it to enhance your performance rather than hinder it. Here's how:

1. **Embrace the Energy:** Recognize that the physical symptoms of anxiety (like increased heart rate) are similar to those of excitement. Shift your perspective to see them as signs that your body is ready to perform.

2. **Focus on the Music:** Direct your attention to the music and the joy of playing. Remind yourself why you love performing and focus on the expressive aspects of your music rather than potential mistakes.

3. **Set Realistic Expectations:** Accept that perfection is not the goal; expressing yourself musically is. Allow room for spontaneity and remember that even professional musicians make mistakes.

4. **Engage with the Audience:** Instead of fearing judgment, view the audience as allies. Engage with them through eye contact and interaction to transform nerves into a shared, positive experience.

5. **Channel Nervous Energy:** Use the adrenaline from nerves to energize your performance. Let it fuel your passion and intensity, enhancing your stage presence and connection with the audience.

In addition to the techniques mentioned, visualization is a powerful tool for overcoming performance nerves. By creating a mental image of a successful performance, you can boost your confidence and prepare your mind for the real event.

1. **Mental Rehearsal:** Spend a few minutes each day visualizing yourself on stage, performing confidently, and receiving positive reactions from your audience.
2. **Focus on the Positive:** Visualize positive outcomes rather than dwelling on potential mistakes.

Regularly practicing visualization and positive imagery, you'll train your mind to associate performing with positive experiences, helping to reduce nerves and enhance your overall stage presence.

By adopting these techniques and reframing your perspective, you'll be better equipped to manage nerves and transform them into a positive force that enhances your live performances.

These skills will enable you to deliver more confident and engaging performances, creating memorable experiences for both you and your audience.

Lesson 21: Setlist Creation

Creating a setlist is a crucial aspect of preparing for a performance. A well-crafted setlist not only showcases your musical abilities but also keeps the audience engaged and entertained. In this lesson, you'll learn how to construct a cohesive setlist that balances energy and flow, ensuring a memorable concert experience.

Crafting a Cohesive Setlist

A cohesive setlist is key to maintaining audience interest throughout your performance. It should guide your listeners on a musical journey, with each song transitioning smoothly into the next. Here are some tips for crafting a cohesive setlist:

- **Start Strong:** Begin with a song that grabs attention and sets the tone for your performance. This could be an energetic opener or a fan favorite that instantly connects with the audience.

The beginning of the set is the most important, as it allows the band to gel into a cohesive musical unit.

- **Consider the Arc:** Think of your setlist as a story with a beginning, middle, and end. Build momentum gradually, leading to a high-energy climax, and then ease into a satisfying conclusion.
- **Balance New and Familiar Material:** Mix familiar songs with new material to keep the audience engaged. Well-known songs can serve as anchors, while new pieces showcase your latest work and creativity.
- **Group Similar Themes:** Arrange songs with similar themes or styles together for a natural flow. This thematic grouping can enhance the overall experience and make the transitions between songs feel seamless.

Balancing Energy and Flow

Balancing energy and flow within your setlist is essential for sustaining audience interest and creating an emotionally dynamic performance. Here's how to achieve this balance:

- **Alternate Tempos:** Vary the tempo of your songs to keep listeners engaged. Follow an upbeat track with a slower, more introspective piece to create contrast and keep the audience engaged.
- **Dynamic Variations:** Incorporate dynamic shifts within your setlist. Alternate between louder, high-energy songs and softer, more subdued ones to add emotional depth and variety.
- **Strategic Placement:** Place high-energy songs at key points in your setlist, such as after a slower ballad or during the climax, to re-energize the audience.
- **Include Audience Participation:** Plan moments for audience interaction, such as sing-alongs or call-and-response sections. This engagement can boost energy levels and create a sense of connection.

By crafting a cohesive setlist that balances energy and flow, you'll deliver a captivating performance that resonates with your audience. These skills are vital for any musician seeking to create memorable, impactful live shows.

Chapter VII Quiz

In this chapter, you learned about performance preparation. Such things as stage presence, overcoming nerves, and creating a stunning setlist.

Q: What is a key component for developing stage confidence?
A: ____

Q: How can you effectively engage with your audience?
A: ____

Q: What technique can help you stay calm on stage?
A: ____

Q: How can you turn anxiety into excitement on stage?
A: ____

Q: What strategy can you use to craft a cohesive setlist?
A: ____

Q: How do you balance energy and flow within a setlist
A: ____

Chapter VII Summary

<u>First</u>, you learn that developing a strong stage presence is crucial for captivating your audience. How you present yourself on stage can make a lasting impression, help you engage your audience, and make them want to come back for more.

<u>Second</u>, developing confidence on stage is key. This comes through rehearsing the set repeatedly and expressing your passion for the message that you're trying to convey.

<u>Third</u>, you learn about how to manage nerves. Performing on stage can be exhilarating, but it can also cause anxiety. Learning strategies to calm your nerves is crucial for any performer to deliver their best on stage.

<u>Fourth</u>, you learn about the importance of creating a solid setlist. This balances the energy and flow of the music, ensuring a memorable concert experience. This is a crucial skill for any performer.

<u>Lastly</u>, plan moments for audience interaction, such as song-alongs or call-and-response sections. This can boost energy levels, create a sense of connection, and make for a memorable performance.

Chapter VIII: Advanced Soloing Concepts

Lesson 22: The Major and Minor Blues Scales

The major and minor blues scales are essential tools for any lead guitarist looking to add depth and emotion to their solos. These scales build on the foundation of the pentatonic scales, introducing additional notes that create a distinctive bluesy feel, rich with expressive possibilities.

In this lesson, we'll explore both the major and minor blues scales, their construction, and how to incorporate them into your playing.

Understanding the Minor Blues Scale

We'll start with the minor blues scale because it is the easiest to play. The minor blues scale is an extension of the minor pentatonic scale, adding a single note that enhances its emotional range.

This scale is widely used in blues, rock, and jazz and is known for its soulful and expressive qualities.

Construction of the Minor Blues Scale

The minor blues scale consists of six notes, derived from the minor pentatonic scale by adding the diminished fifth (also known as the "blue note") You extend the pentatonic scale, and you create a more bluesy, moody tone.

A Minor Scale: A B C D E F G = 7 notes

A Minor Pentatonic: A C D E G = 5 notes

A Minor Blues Scale: A C D Eb E G = 6 notes

Technically, the minor blues scale is made up of the root, minor third, perfect fourth, diminished fifth (blue note), perfect fifth, and a minor seventh.

Or, the root, flat 3rd, perfect 4th, flat 5th, perfect 5th, and the flat 7th. By adding this "blue" note, you create a different shade of color. A great way to enhance your soloing vocabulary.

Let's look at a few ways to use this scale in your music compositions.

Using the Minor Blues Scale

- **Expressive Solos:** Utilize the blue note to add tension and release within your solos. This can create a more emotional and dynamic performance.
- **Bending and Slides:** Incorporate bends and slides to emphasize the blue note, bringing out its unique sound and enhancing your expressive capabilities.
- **Blues Licks:** Learn and incorporate classic blues licks that utilize the minor blues scale. These can serve as building blocks for your solos.

Exploring the Major Blues Scale

The major blues scale, though less commonly discussed, offers a bright and uplifting sound, perfect for adding variety to your musical palette. It's particularly effective in genres like country, jazz, and rock.

C Major Scale: C D E F G A B = 7 notes

C Major Pentatonic: C D E G A = 5 notes

C Major Blues Scale: C D Eb E G A = 6 notes

As with the minor blues scale, you add the 'blue" note. But in the major blues scale, you add it in the 3rd position. The minor third note.

Technically, this scale is made up of the root, major second, minor third, major third, perfect fifth, and major sixth.

Or the root, 2nd, flat 3rd, 3rd, 5th, and 6th. Six notes that allow you to create a different shade of color.

Using the Major Blues Scale

- **Lively Melodies:** Use the major blues scale to craft vibrant, joyful melodies, adding a fresh twist to your solos.
- **Improvisational Freedom:** The scale's structure allows for creative improvisation, enabling you to explore new musical ideas and expressions.
- **Contrast in Solos:** Incorporate the major blues scale alongside the minor blues scale within your solos to create contrast and keep listeners engaged.

Incorporating Blues Scales into Your Playing

- **Practice Exercises:** Devote time to practicing both scales across different keys and positions on the fretboard. This will increase your familiarity and fluency.

- **Jam with Backing Tracks:** Use blues backing tracks to practice improvising with these scales. This context helps you understand how the scales interact with chord progressions.

- **Analyze Blues Solos:** Study solos from renowned blues guitarists to see how they utilize these scales. This analysis can provide insight into effective phrasing and application.

Focus on these concepts when using the blues scales. They will allow you to not only craft memorable melody lines but also increase your mastery over the fretboard.

Finger Exercises For Dexterity Development

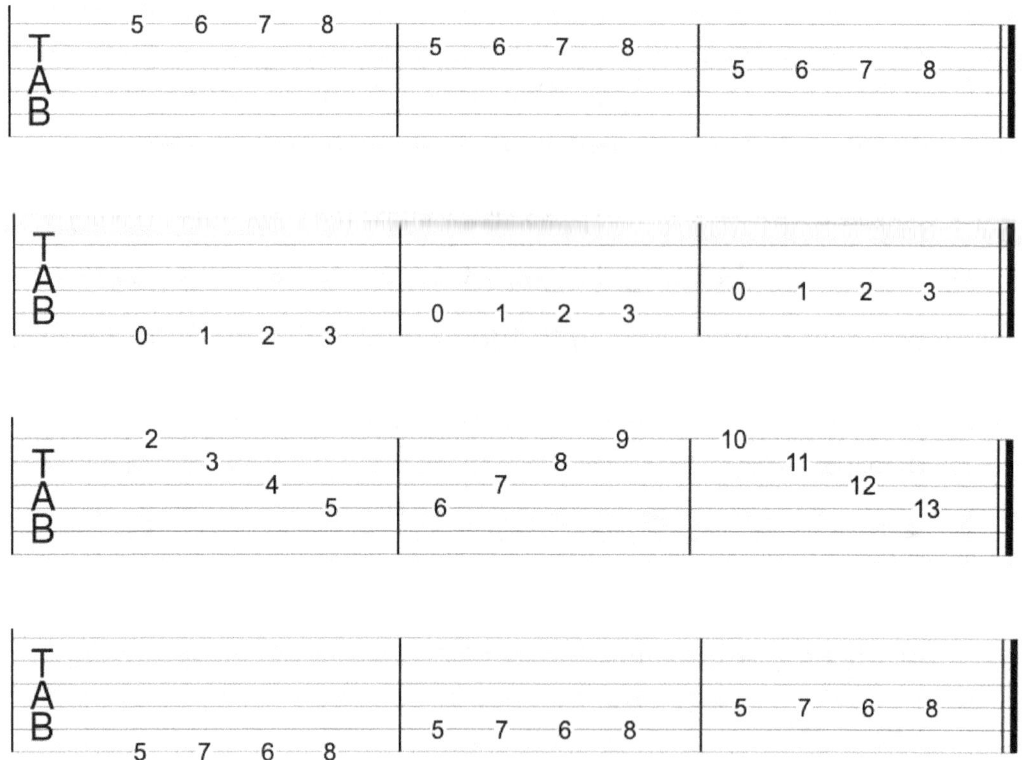

By mastering the major and minor blues scales, you'll expand your expressive toolkit and enhance your ability to craft emotive, impactful solos. These scales are not only foundational to the blues genre but also versatile tools for a wide array of musical styles. Embrace the rich, expressive potential they offer, and enjoy the creative journey they unlock.

Lesson 23: Sweep Picking Arpeggios

Sweep picking is a powerful technique that allows you to play arpeggios with incredible speed and fluidity. This technique involves a smooth, sweeping motion of the pick across the strings, enabling you to execute complex arpeggio patterns efficiently.

Mastering sweep picking can elevate your lead guitar playing, adding impressive technical flair to your solos and compositions.

Understanding Sweep Picking

Sweep picking is a method where the pick moves in a single, continuous motion across multiple strings, as opposed to the traditional down-up alternate picking. This technique allows rapid execution of arpeggios by minimizing movement of the pick hand.

- **Sweep Technique:** The fundamental aspect of sweep picking is the smooth, fluid motion of the pick. As you play through an arpeggio, the pick should glide across the strings in one continuous direction, either down (for descending arpeggios) or up (for ascending arpeggios).

- **Finger Coordination:** While your picking hand executes the sweeping motion, your fretting hand must coordinate precisely to articulate each note cleanly. This requires synchronized finger movements to ensure clarity and prevent unwanted string noise.

Basic Sweep Picking Exercises

Before tackling complex arpeggios, it's essential to build a strong foundation through basic sweep-picking exercises. Here are some ideas to get you started:

1. **Three-String Arpeggios:** Begin with simple three-string arpeggios, such as primary and minor triads. Focus on maintaining a consistent sweep motion and clear note articulation.

- ○ **Primary Triad Example:** Practice a three-string major triad starting on the high E string, sweeping down from the G string to the high E string.
- ○ **Minor Triad Example:** Apply the same technique to a minor triad, ensuring each note rings clearly.

2. **Four-String Arpeggios:** Once comfortable with three-string patterns, expand to four-string arpeggios. This will challenge your coordination and help develop greater control.

   - ○ **Exercise:** Practice a four-string arpeggio, such as a diminished or augmented arpeggio, sweeping smoothly from the D string to the high E string.

3. **Economy of Motion:** Focus on minimizing unnecessary pick movement and maintaining a relaxed wrist. This economy of motion is crucial for achieving speed and precision.

Arpeggio Exercises for Daily Practice

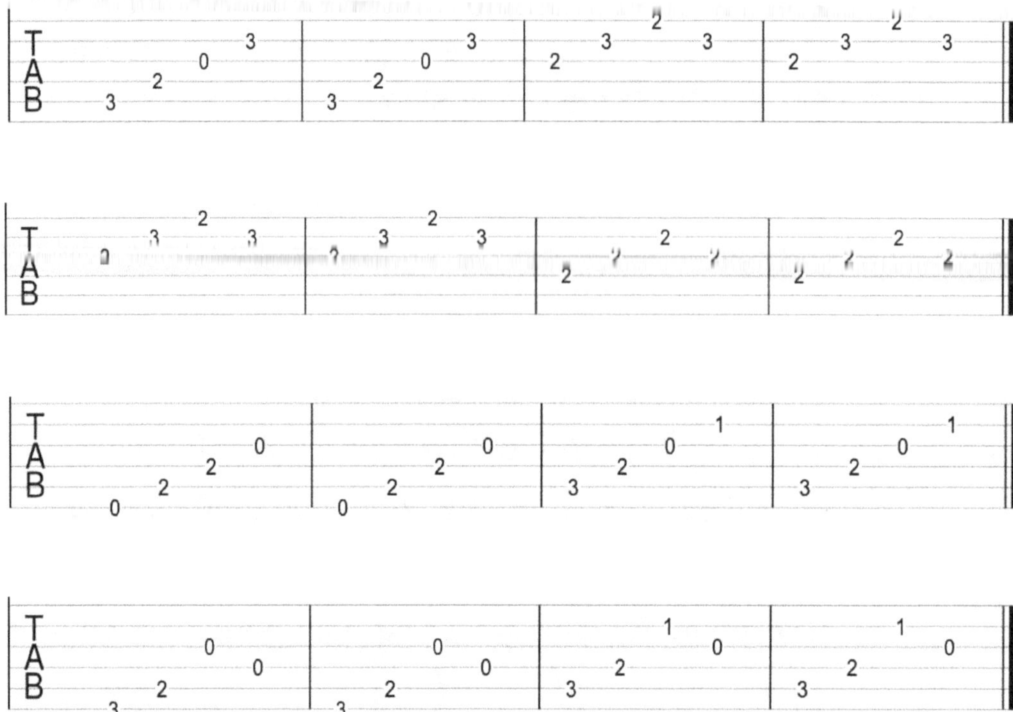

Notice how these all start on different strings. This gives you a chance to get familiar with basic chords and this area of the fretboard.

Make sure you start slowly and focus on playing the notes with clarity, as this will be highly important as you increase speed over time.

Advanced Sweep Picking Techniques

Once you've mastered the basics, explore more advanced sweep picking techniques to enhance your playing further:

- **Five- and Six-String Arpeggios:** Gradually incorporate five- and six-string arpeggios into your practice. These extended patterns offer more musical possibilities and challenge your technical proficiency.

- **Tapping and Legato Integration:** Combine sweep picking with tapping and legato techniques to create intricate, flowing lines. These combinations can add complexity and expressiveness to your arpeggios.

- **Dynamic Variations:** Experiment with dynamics by varying the pressure and speed of your sweeps. This can add emotional depth and contrast to your playing.

- **String Skipping:** Incorporate string-skipping into your sweep-picking patterns for added complexity and a unique sound. This technique involves skipping one or more strings between notes, creating wider intervals and interesting melodic lines.

Practice Tips for Mastering Sweep Picking

- **Start Slow:** Begin at a slow tempo to ensure accuracy and clarity. Gradually increase speed as you gain confidence and precision.
- **Use a Metronome:** Practice with a metronome to maintain consistent timing and build rhythmic stability.
- **Focus on Cleanliness:** Pay attention to muting techniques to prevent unwanted string noise. Use your palm or fingers to mute adjacent strings as needed.
- **Record Your Practice:** Regularly record your sweep picking exercises to monitor progress and identify areas for improvement.

By mastering sweep picking arpeggios, you'll gain the ability to execute rapid, complex patterns with ease and confidence. These skills will enhance your lead guitar playing.

This allows you to craft solos that impress with both speed and musicality. Embrace the challenge of sweep picking and enjoy the creative possibilities it brings to your musical journey.

Lesson 24: Finger Tapping and Legato

Finger tapping and legato are advanced techniques that can add impressive flair and fluidity to your guitar playing. These techniques allow for rapid note sequences and smooth transitions, making your solos more dynamic and expressive.

Mastering Finger Tapping

Finger tapping involves using your picking hand to "tap" notes on the fretboard, creating seamless, fast passages that can extend your playing range.

- **Basic Technique:** Start by holding the pick between your thumb and index finger, using your middle or ring finger to tap the fretboard. Tap down firmly on a fret to sound the note without plucking the string.

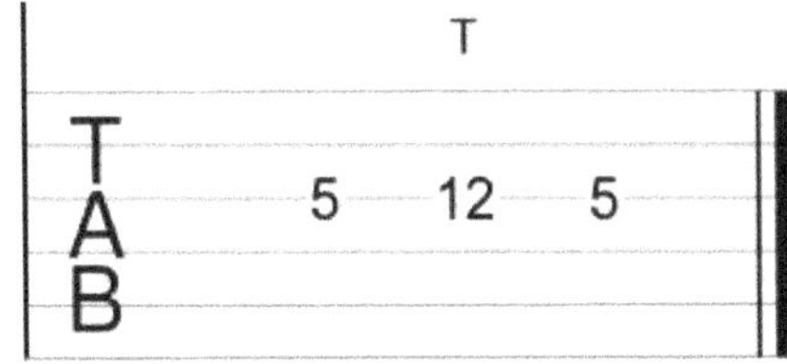

In this example, you pick the 5th fret, tap on the 12th fret, then choose the 12th fret again.

- **Two-Handed Tapping:** Combine tapping with your fretting hand to create more complex phrases. Alternate between tapping and hammering-on with your fretting hand to achieve fluid, cascading lines.
- **Practice Patterns:** Begin with simple exercises, such as tapping a note on the high E string and pulling off to a lower note. Gradually increase complexity by incorporating multiple strings and faster tempos.

Finger Tapping Examples

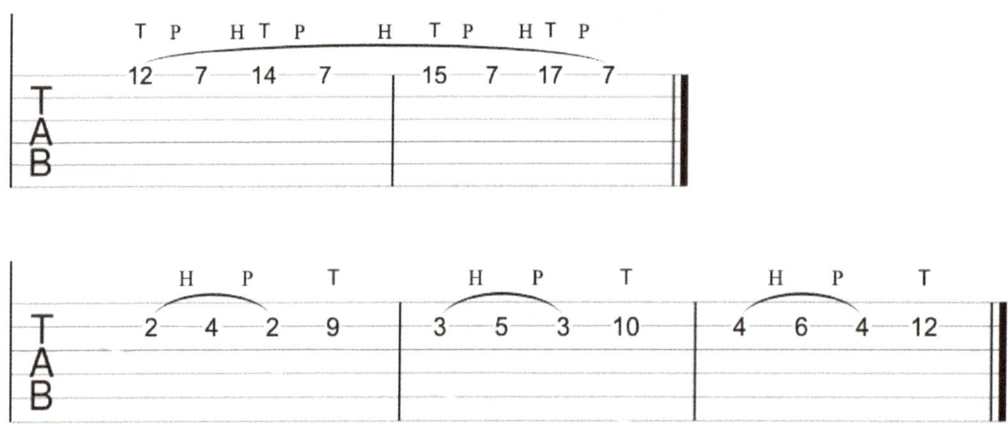

Practice these daily to get familiar wth this technique. These will allow you to explore advanced levels of play.

Exploring Legato Techniques

Legato playing involves smooth, connected notes achieved through hammer-ons and pull-offs, minimizing the use of the picking hand. This technique contributes to a fluid, seamless sound.

- **Hammer-Ons:** Start by picking a note, then "hammer" onto a higher fret with one of your fingers without re-picking the string. This technique allows for rapid note sequences.
- **Pull-Offs:** Play a note and then "pull off" to a lower note by flicking the string with your fretting finger. Ensure the pulled-off note rings clearly and with equal volume.
- **Combining Techniques:** Practice combining hammer-ons and pull-offs to create continuous legato runs. Focus on maintaining even timing and volume across all notes.

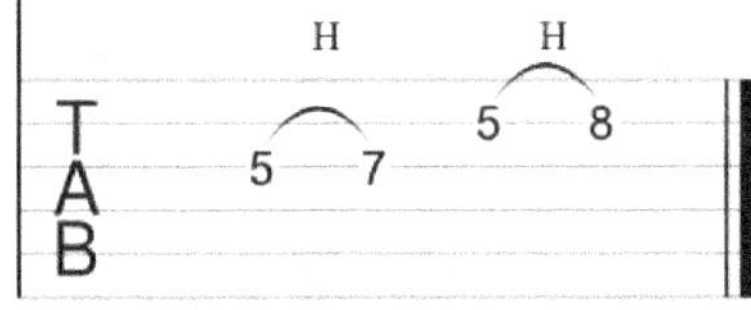

A double hammer-on legato run. Pick the first note only.

Integrating Tapping and Legato

By integrating finger tapping and legato, you can achieve impressive speed and expression in your solos.

- **Complex Runs:** Create intricate runs by combining tapping with legato phrases. This technique allows for extended musical lines that flow effortlessly across the fretboard.
- **Speed Building:** Use these techniques to build speed while maintaining clarity. Start slowly, focusing on precision, and gradually increase the tempo as you become more comfortable.
- **Expressive Phrasing:** Incorporate tapping and legato into your solos to add expressiveness and flair. These techniques allow for rapid embellishments and creative phrasing that captivate listeners.

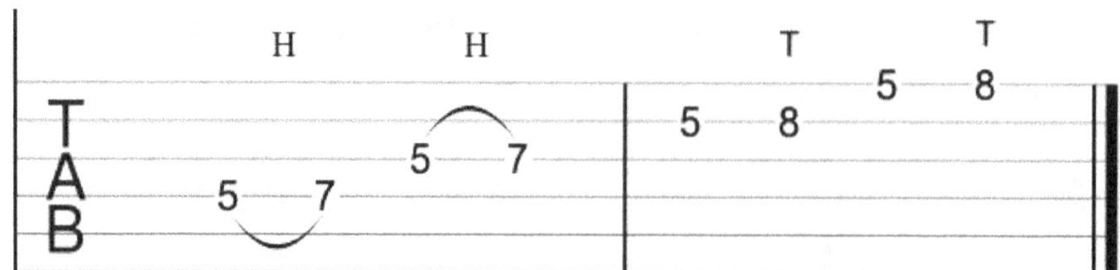

In this example, you do a legato run tap.

Practice Tips for Tapping and Legato

- **Metronome Practice:** Use a metronome to help with timing and consistency. Begin at a slow tempo and gradually increase speed as you develop confidence.
- **Muting Techniques:** Use your palm or fingers to mute unwanted string noise. Clean execution is crucial for maintaining clarity, especially during fast passages.
- **Experiment with Dynamics:** Vary the pressure and speed of your tapping and legato to explore different dynamics and emotional effects.
- **Record and Review:** Regularly record your practice sessions to monitor progress and refine your technique.

By mastering finger tapping and legato, you'll add a new dimension to your guitar playing, enabling you to execute rapid, fluid solos with ease. These techniques will enhance your ability to express creativity and emotion through your music, leaving a lasting impression on your audience.

Embrace the challenge of tapping and legato, and explore the exciting possibilities they bring to your musical journey.

Lesson 25. Effective Practice Habits

Developing effective practice habits is essential for any guitarist aspiring to improve their skills and reach their musical goals. Consistent and focused practice allows you to make meaningful progress, build muscle memory, and refine your technique.

In this chapter, we will explore strategies for creating a productive practice routine that maximizes your potential and keeps you motivated.

Establishing a Routine

Creating a structured practice routine is the cornerstone of effective learning. A well-organized schedule helps you stay on track and ensures that you cover all necessary areas of improvement.

- **Set Clear Goals:** Define specific, achievable goals for each practice session. Whether it's mastering a new scale, improving your speed, or learning a new song, having a clear objective gives your practice purpose and direction.

- **Allocate Time Wisely:** Divide your practice time into focused segments, dedicating time to various aspects such as scales, technique exercises, improvisation, and repertoire. This approach ensures balanced skill development and keeps your sessions dynamic.
- **Consistency is Key:** Aim to practice regularly, even if it's for shorter durations. Consistent daily practice is more effective than sporadic, lengthy sessions. This consistency helps reinforce learning and builds muscle memory.

Effective Practice Techniques

Incorporating effective practice techniques can accelerate your progress and enhance your learning experience. Here are some methods to consider:

- **Slow Practice:** Begin new pieces or difficult sections at a slow tempo. This allows you to focus on accuracy and technique without rushing. Gradually increase the speed as you become more comfortable.

- **Focused Repetition:** Practice challenging passages repeatedly, but with attention to detail. Repetition helps solidify muscle memory, but make sure to correct mistakes immediately to avoid ingraining errors.

- **Metronome Use:** Use a metronome to develop a strong sense of timing and rhythm. Start at a comfortable tempo and gradually increase the speed as you gain confidence and precision.

- **Record and Review:** Regularly record your practice sessions to assess your progress objectively. Listening back can help you identify areas for improvement and track your development over time.

Staying Motivated

Maintaining motivation and enthusiasm is crucial for sustaining long-term practice. Here are some tips to keep you inspired:

- **Set Milestones:** Break down long-term goals into smaller milestones. Celebrate each achievement to maintain a sense of accomplishment and motivation.
- **Vary Your Practice:** Keep your practice sessions interesting by incorporating a variety of exercises and musical styles. This diversity prevents boredom and encourages creativity.
- **Seek Inspiration:** Listen to your favorite guitarists and explore different genres to find new sources of inspiration. Attend live performances or watch online videos to reignite your passion for music.
- **Join a Community:** Engage with fellow musicians through jam sessions, online forums, or local music groups. Sharing your journey with others can provide support, encouragement, and new insights.

Practice Routine

- **Warm-Up and Technique Development (15 minutes):** Start your practice session with a focused warm-up to get your fingers moving and your mind engaged. Begin with basic finger exercises, such as scales, chromatic runs, alternate picking, and tremolo picking, to improve finger agility and coordination.

- **Creative Improvisation and Exploration (20 minutes):** Focus on exploring different scales and modes, such as the pentatonic or blues scales, to develop your musical vocabulary. Experiment with incorporating techniques like bends, slides, and hammer-ons to add expressiveness to your solos.

By cultivating effective practice habits and a solid practice routine, you'll set yourself on a path of continuous growth and improvement.

Enhance your technical abilities and deepen your connection to the music by expressing yourself more fully and confidently. Remember, practice is not just about repetition; it's about intentional, focused, and disciplined learning.

Chapter VIII Quiz

In this chapter, you learned about advanced soloing concepts. First, starting with the blues scales, sweep picking arpeggios, finger tapping, legato, and finally, effective practice habits.

Q: What additional note is used to make the minor blues?
A: ____

Q: How can the major blues scale enhance your solos?
A; ____

Q: What is the primary advantage of using sweep picking?
A: ____

Q: What are the techniques used in finger tapping?
A: ____

Q: How can legato be beneficial to your guitar solos?
A; ____

Q: What makes an effective practice routine for improvement?
A: ____

Chapter VIII Summary

First, you learn about the major and minor blues scales and how they are vital tools for lead guitarists. They allow you to add an additional note to the pentatonics that creates a distinctive bluesy feel

<u>Second</u>, you discover this additional note is called the "blue" note, and it is a way to not only change the emotion of the scale, but also extend your knowledge of the fretboard.

<u>Third</u>, you learn about sweep picking. A powerful technique that allows you to play arpeggios with speed and fluidity. Involving a smooth sweep picking technique across the strings.

<u>Fourth</u>, finger tapping and legato are advanced techniques that add flair to your playing. These utilize rapid note sequences and smooth transitions, making your solos more dynamic and expressive.

<u>Lastly</u>, you learn about effective practice habits. Consistent and focused daily practice is needed for meaningful progress, building muscle memory, and fretboard mastery. Expressing yourself more confidently.

Pentatonic Scales: Conclusion

As we conclude, it is best to reflect on the journey you've taken. *Learn to Play the Pentatonic Scales* has provided you with a comprehensive roadmap to mastering the art of lead guitar playing.

To continue your growth as a guitarist, remember that consistent practice and exploration are key. Regularly engaging with a variety of musical styles and listening to diverse guitarists will broaden your musical horizons and inspire new ideas.

As you progress on your musical journey, embrace each challenge as an opportunity for growth and discovery. Your dedication and passion for the guitar will undoubtedly lead to rewarding experiences and meaningful connections.

Throughout the chapters, you've explored the versatile pentatonic scale, essential techniques, and the importance of rhythm and timing. Delving into the intricacies of bending, vibrato, and other expressive techniques that add depth and emotion to your playing.

Remember that mastery is a journey, not a destination. Stay curious, be patient with yourself, and embrace the challenges that come with learning and growing as a musician. Your dedication and passion for the guitar will undoubtedly lead to rewarding and fulfilling musical experiences.

Your growth as a guitarist doesn't end here. Continual practice and exploration are crucial for honing your skills. Here are some practical tips to support your ongoing development:

- **Regular Practice:** Set aside dedicated practice time each day to reinforce techniques and explore new musical ideas.
- **Listen Actively:** Immerse yourself in a wide range of music. Analyze the work of various guitarists to draw inspiration and expand your musical vocabulary.

Thank you for embarking on this journey. May your guitar playing continue to evolve, and may your music inspire and connect with audiences around the world.

To all your success,
Sincerely, Dwayne Jenkins

Other Books From Dwayne Jenkins

Learn Guitar Scale Theory:

Dive deep into guitar scale theory with this easy to learn from, comprehensive guidebook. An understanding of theory can add a rich vocabulary for both harmony and melody.

Learn Guitar Scale Theory will help you expand your improvisation skills, enhance your scale vocabulary, and deepen your understanding of intervals.

Learn To Play Rhythm Guitar:

A comprehensive training course for learning chords, chord progressions, strumming, arpeggiated picking, and all things needed to be a great rhythm guitar player.

With a step-by-step system and your desire to learn, you'll be playing quickly and easily. Before you know it, you will increase your musicianship and understanding of timing and rhythm.

Learn Guitar Chord Theory:

Have you ever looked at notation and wondered what a Cadd9 chord is? Or possibly a Gsus4? If you have, this book will explain what it is, how to create it, and how to use it.

Learn Guitar Chord Theory is a comprehensive study guide on the inner workings of guitar chords. Take the time to develop your chord vocabulary and mix it with a complete understanding of how they work, and you'll become a much better player.

124

All books are authored by Dwayne Jenkins, published by Tritone Publishing, and are available worldwide.

Digital formats of all titles are also available for quicker learning. Just download them onto your computer and start learning right away.

Self-study is a great way to learn, as it allows you not only to go at your own pace but also to develop self-discipline and time management, which can benefit you in other areas of your life.

Also, check out Dwayne's Guitar Lessons video channel on YouTube. These are free lessons that cover a wide variety of topics related to playing the guitar.

Whether you are working on rhythm, lead, theory, or guitar maintenance, it is all here in these lessons. These are available 24 hours a day, 7 days a week, 365 days a year.

And if more help is needed, Dwayne also offers one-on-one private coaching, available on his website.

DwaynesGuitarLessons.com

Best of luck, and have fun.

About the Author

Dwayne Jenkins is a professional guitar teacher, an accomplished musician, and an entrepreneur. He has been learning, playing, and teaching guitar lessons throughout Denver, CO, for over two decades.

He is now bringing his special training skills and methodology, honed and hand-crafted over the years, to help students around the world play.

Dwayne has a unique, exciting approach that gets students of all ages and skill levels enjoying the fun of playing guitar and ukulele. His enthusiasm and love for teaching shine through every lesson that he creates.

His lessons are designed to help you progress. No matter your reason for learning, there will always be something in Dwayne's books and products to help you achieve your dreams.

So if you're a student looking to start or a student looking to further your education, be sure to get involved with Dwayne's guitar lessons and learn what so many people have already discovered: why learning to play the guitar is one of the most incredible things you can do for yourself.

What Students Are Saying About Dwayne's Guitar Lessons

"Dwayne, thank you so much for everything you have taught me and done for me. You are an amazing guitarist and wonderful teacher." R.I

"Dwayne, it has been a true pleasure to have you at our house each week! Ken & Trevor have learned so much through you and your teachings. Thank you!" Lisa

"Dwayne, thank you for being a great teacher and teaching me many great songs. This is a skill that will last me a lifetime." Danielle

"Dwayne, we want you to know we are honored to have you at the studio. We appreciate all that you do and are grateful that we can leave you in charge." Angie & Wilson M.E.C.

"Dwayne, we are so glad you are our Teacher. It's been three years already, can you believe it? Thank you again. You're the best!" Chelsey & Lucas.

"Dwayne, we are so glad that you are in our lives. Chelsey & Lucas enjoy their time with you and look up to you. Looking forward to another great year!" Love and best wishes, Ken & Sue.

"Dwayne, thank you so much for being not only an awesome guitar teacher but an awesome friend as well," Kayla said.

"Dwayne, thank you so much for all the years of doing lessons. You have been very patient with my progress, helped me to build confidence in myself, and inspired me to follow my dreams. And in doing so, you have become a great friend." Jake.

"Dwayne, thank you for teaching Nick guitar so well. He loves it and is getting quite good fast. I'm amazed!" Jane.

"Dwayne, thank you so much for teaching me every Saturday, and not only teaching me guitar but also about life and helping me with setting my goals. You are a great teacher, mentor, and the best friend ever." Carson.

"There is no other person I would want to teach me a guitar! His 1-on-1 teaching makes learning guitar very personal & exhilarating. He teaches at your pace and takes pride in what YOU want to learn. The best part is that if Dwayne doesn't know a song a student wants to play, he takes time out of the week to learn it. His teaching comes to life in my performance and has progressed over the last 8 years. Words cannot describe how amazing a teacher, rockstar, and true friend Dwayne has become to me." Dominic.

Resource Guide

The Five Major Pentatonic Scales

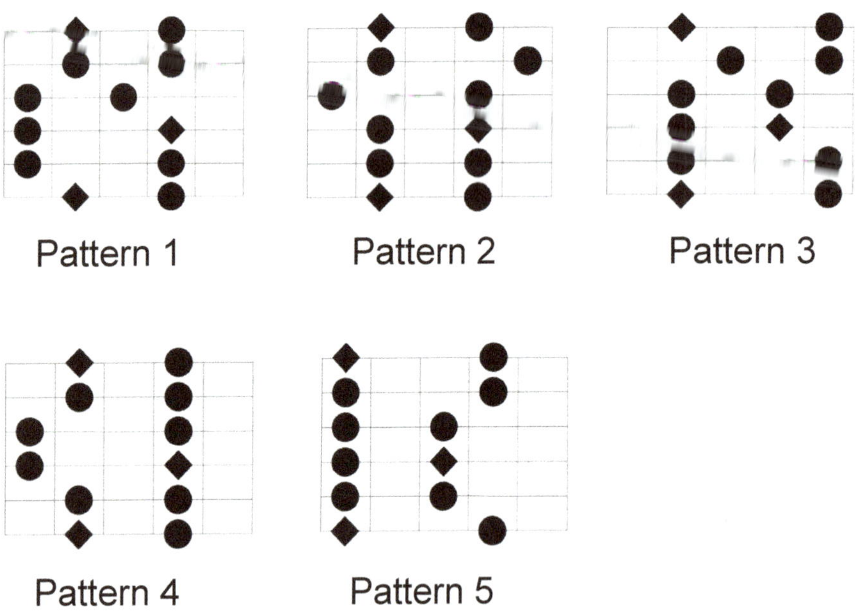

Pattern 1   Pattern 2   Pattern 3

Pattern 4   Pattern 5

Things to remember:

1. It is a five-note scale that produces a bright, happy sound.
2. The number value is 1 2 3 5 6.
3. Key Example, C Major: C D E G A
4. Created by eliminating the 4th and 7th notes of the major.
5. Each pattern starts on a tone degree of the scale.

The Five Minor Pentatonic Scales

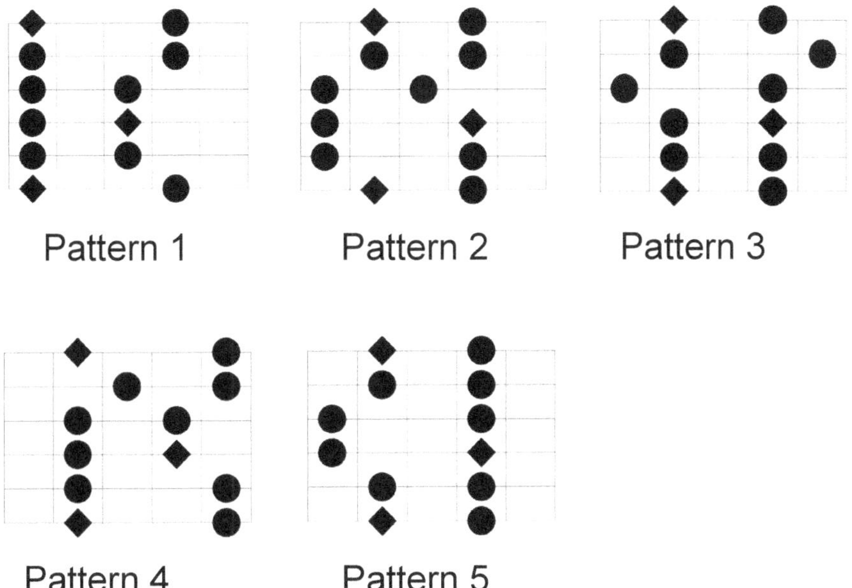

Pattern 1   Pattern 2   Pattern 3

Pattern 4   Pattern 5

1. It is a five-note scale that produces a sad, somber sound.
2. The number value is 1 b3 4 5 b7
3. Key example, A minor: A C D E G
4. Created by eliminating the 2nd and 6th of the major.
5. Each pattern starts on a tone degree of the scale.

These five-note scale patterns are essential for lead guitar mastery. Once you get these down, move on to mastering the blues scales and the modes.

Although simple, do not overlook their potency. They are used by all the great blues and rock guitar players.